Agricultural Ecosystem-Based Solutions: Supporting Soil Health, Regenerative Farming, Biodiversity, Water Conservation, Climate Resilience, and Sustainable Agriculture

Copyright

Agricultural Ecosystem-Based Solutions: Supporting Soil Health, Regenerative Farming, Biodiversity, Water Conservation, Climate Resilience, and Sustainable Agriculture

© 2025 Robert C. Brears

ISBN (eBook): 978-1-991368-13-3

ISBN (Paperback): 978-1-991368-14-0

Published by Global Climate Solutions

First Edition, 2025

Cover design and interior layout by Global Climate Solutions

Table of Contents

Introduction

Agricultural ecosystems are at the center of some of humanity's greatest challenges and opportunities. As the world's population grows and pressures mount on land, water, and biodiversity, there is a rising need to reimagine how food is produced in a way that maintains ecological balance while supporting livelihoods. Ecosystem-based solutions (EBS) in agriculture offer a promising pathway toward resilient, sustainable, and productive food systems by working with, rather than against, nature's processes.

EBS are grounded in the understanding that agricultural landscapes provide not only food, fiber, and fuel, but also a range of vital ecosystem services—such as nutrient cycling, water regulation, soil formation, pollination, and pest control. These functions are essential for the long-term sustainability of farming systems and for the well-being of rural and urban communities alike. Conventional agricultural practices, focused primarily on maximizing short-term yields, have often degraded these services through monocultures, excessive input use, and habitat loss. This has resulted in soil erosion, declining water quality, biodiversity loss, and increased vulnerability to climate change.

Transitioning toward ecosystem-based approaches represents a fundamental shift in mindset and management. It requires recognizing the interconnectedness of agricultural practices with broader ecological processes, and valuing the diversity, connectivity, and adaptive capacity of landscapes. Practices such as cover cropping, crop rotation, reduced tillage, agroforestry, integrated pest management (IPM), and the restoration of natural habitats contribute to regenerative agriculture. These strategies enhance soil health, conserve water, support beneficial organisms, and reduce dependence on synthetic inputs, all while maintaining or improving productivity.

Key to the success of EBS in agriculture is the application of core ecological principles. Diversity—both in the crops grown and in the life present in soils—fosters resilience and stability. Connectivity, through features like buffer strips, hedgerows, and ecological corridors, supports the flow of species and ecosystem functions. The health and vitality of soils, as living ecosystems in themselves, underpin the productivity and adaptability of entire farming systems. Adaptive management—responding to environmental feedback and changing conditions—ensures that these systems remain effective over time.

The adoption of EBS is not without challenges. Barriers include entrenched conventional practices, economic and informational constraints, and gaps in policy and institutional support. Addressing these requires collaborative action from farmers, researchers, extension services, policymakers, and communities. Empowering local knowledge, supporting innovation, and creating enabling environments are all vital for the transition.

This book provides a comprehensive exploration of EBS in agriculture, highlighting their principles, practices, and benefits. It emphasizes the potential of EBS to transform agricultural landscapes into multifunctional systems that deliver food security, climate resilience, biodiversity conservation, and social well-being. By working with nature, agriculture can not only meet the demands of today but also ensure the sustainability and health of food systems for generations to come.

Chapter 1: Foundations Of Ecosystem-Based Solutions in Agriculture

Chapter 1 lays the groundwork for understanding EBS in agriculture by exploring the fundamental ecological principles that sustain productive, resilient, and sustainable food systems. Agriculture is deeply intertwined with natural processes, from nutrient cycling and soil formation to water regulation and biodiversity. This chapter examines how these ecosystem services function within agricultural landscapes and why recognizing their value is crucial for long-term viability. It highlights the differences between conventional and ecosystem-based approaches, showing how EBS leverage natural cycles, diversity, and adaptive management to support both productivity and environmental health. The discussion sets the stage for a holistic view of farming—one that integrates agroecology, multifunctionality, and stewardship. By grounding the conversation in science and practical experience, Chapter 1 provides the essential context for adopting and scaling EBS across a range of farming systems and landscapes.

Understanding Ecosystem Services in Agricultural Landscapes

Ecosystem services are the benefits people derive from nature's processes, and within agricultural landscapes, these services underpin the productivity, sustainability, and resilience of food systems. Agricultural lands, while managed primarily for crop or livestock production, simultaneously provide and depend upon a range of ecosystem functions—such as soil formation, nutrient cycling, water regulation, pollination, and pest control. Understanding these services is fundamental for designing agricultural systems that work with, rather than against, nature.

Provisioning services, such as food, fiber, and fuel, are the most obvious outputs of agriculture, but supporting services—like soil fertility, microbial activity, and nutrient recycling—form the unseen foundation of farm productivity. Regulating services include the purification of water, climate moderation, flood control, and disease suppression. Pollinators, natural predators, and healthy soils all contribute to these processes, reducing the need for external inputs and enhancing system stability. Cultural services, though less tangible, are also significant, as agricultural landscapes contribute to heritage, recreation, and aesthetic values that benefit communities.

Modern agriculture has often focused on maximizing provisioning services at the expense of others, leading to ecosystem degradation, loss of biodiversity, and declining resilience. Recognizing the interconnectedness of ecosystem services means understanding the trade-offs and synergies that exist within managed landscapes. Enhancing supporting and regulating services—such as through maintaining habitat diversity, restoring riparian buffers, or integrating trees—can help agriculture become more productive and sustainable over time.

By valuing and actively managing ecosystem services, farmers and land managers can build resilience to environmental shocks, reduce dependency on costly inputs, and secure long-term productivity. This ecosystem-based perspective encourages practices that sustain natural capital, such as cover cropping, agroforestry, and rotational grazing. In this way, agricultural landscapes can be both productive and regenerative, ensuring that the essential services upon which food systems depend are preserved and enhanced for future generations.

Ecological Principles Underpinning EBS

The ecological principles that underpin EBS in agriculture are grounded in the understanding that healthy ecosystems sustain productive and resilient farming systems. Central to EBS is the concept of working with natural processes rather than attempting to override them. This approach relies on fostering ecological balance, maintaining diversity, and supporting the dynamic interactions among soil, water, plants, animals, and microorganisms.

One core principle is diversity, both above and below ground. Diverse cropping systems and landscapes promote resilience by providing habitat for beneficial organisms, spreading risk, and supporting complex food webs. Crop rotations, intercropping, and polycultures mimic natural systems, helping to interrupt pest cycles, reduce disease outbreaks, and maintain soil fertility. Below the surface, diverse soil communities drive nutrient cycling and improve soil structure, supporting plant health and productivity.

Another key principle is connectivity. By maintaining ecological corridors, buffer zones, and patches of natural vegetation, farms can facilitate the movement of species, genes, and resources. This connectivity ensures pollination, pest regulation, and genetic exchange, supporting the adaptive capacity of agricultural systems to respond to changing environmental conditions.

EBS also emphasize the principle of ecological redundancy. By incorporating multiple species that provide similar functions—such as different types of nitrogen-fixing plants or various predators of crop pests—systems become less vulnerable to disturbance. If one species is lost, others can maintain critical functions, enhancing overall system stability.

Soil health is foundational to EBS, relying on the principle of sustaining living soils. Practices that increase soil organic matter, protect soil cover, and minimize disturbance help to build soil structure, retain water, and support diverse microbial life. These conditions improve plant growth, nutrient cycling, and resilience to drought or heavy rainfall.

Finally, adaptive management is essential, recognizing that ecosystems are dynamic and constantly changing. EBS in agriculture require ongoing observation, learning, and adjustment to respond to feedback from the environment. By embracing these ecological principles—diversity, connectivity, redundancy, healthy soils, and adaptation—EBS create agricultural systems that are productive, sustainable, and capable of withstanding environmental change.

Transitioning From Conventional to Ecosystem-Based Approaches

Transitioning from conventional agricultural practices to ecosystem-based approaches involves a fundamental shift in mindset and management. Conventional systems often focus on maximizing short-term yields through the intensive use of synthetic fertilizers, pesticides, and monocultures. While these methods can increase production, they frequently degrade natural resources, reduce biodiversity, and leave farms vulnerable to pests, diseases, and climate variability. Moving toward EBS requires rethinking how agricultural landscapes are designed and managed to prioritize long-term productivity, ecological health, and resilience.

The transition begins with an assessment of existing practices and their impacts on soil, water, and biodiversity. This process involves identifying areas of degradation—such as eroded soils, polluted waterways, or declining pollinator populations—and understanding how current management contributes to these issues. Farmers and land managers are encouraged to adopt a holistic perspective, recognizing the interconnectedness of different components within the farming system and the broader landscape.

Implementing EBS involves integrating practices that restore ecosystem functions and services. This may include diversifying crop rotations, incorporating cover crops, reducing tillage, establishing hedgerows or buffer strips, and adopting IPM. These changes not only enhance ecosystem health but also reduce reliance on external inputs, making farms more self-sustaining and cost-effective over time.

Transitioning to EBS is rarely a one-size-fits-all process. It requires tailoring solutions to specific environmental, social, and economic contexts. Engaging with local knowledge, experimenting with new practices on a small scale, and gradually scaling up successful approaches can facilitate adoption and reduce risks. Support from agricultural extension services, peer learning, and access to technical and financial resources are also critical for enabling change.

Ultimately, shifting to ecosystem-based approaches represents an investment in the long-term viability of agriculture. By embracing ecological principles and prioritizing sustainability, farms can become more productive, resilient, and better equipped to face the challenges of a changing world. The transition is a journey that rewards innovation, collaboration, and a commitment to stewardship of both land and natural resources.

The Role of Agroecology and Sustainable Agriculture

Agroecology and sustainable agriculture form the backbone of EBS in farming systems, emphasizing a holistic approach that integrates ecological science with practical management. Agroecology applies principles from ecology to agricultural production, promoting practices that enhance biodiversity, support ecosystem services, and build resilience to environmental stresses. It focuses on understanding the interactions between plants, animals, soil, climate, and human communities, viewing the farm as an integrated system within its landscape context.

Sustainable agriculture, closely aligned with agroecology, prioritizes the long-term health of both people and the environment. It seeks to balance food production with the preservation of natural resources, ensuring that soil fertility, water quality, and biodiversity are maintained or enhanced over time. Sustainable systems minimize reliance on synthetic chemicals, optimize resource use efficiency, and encourage the recycling of nutrients and organic matter within the farm.

Both agroecology and sustainable agriculture advocate for diversified cropping systems, including intercropping, crop rotations, agroforestry, and the integration of livestock. These strategies mimic natural ecosystems, fostering functional diversity that regulates pests, improves soil structure, and enhances pollination. By supporting beneficial organisms and reducing the prevalence of pests and diseases, these systems can decrease the need for chemical interventions.

Social equity and knowledge sharing are also central to agroecology and sustainable agriculture. Farmers, communities, and local stakeholders are encouraged to participate in decision-making, drawing on traditional knowledge and local innovations alongside scientific research. This participatory approach empowers rural communities, builds capacity for adaptation, and ensures that agricultural practices are well-suited to local conditions.

Adopting agroecological and sustainable agriculture practices leads to farming systems that are productive, resilient, and capable of adapting to change. These approaches help secure food production while restoring ecosystem health, supporting rural livelihoods, and contributing to the broader goals of environmental sustainability and social well-being. As the world faces growing pressures on food systems and natural resources, agroecology and sustainable agriculture provide essential frameworks for advancing EBS in agriculture.

Multifunctionality of Agricultural Systems

Multifunctionality in agricultural systems refers to the capacity of farming landscapes to provide a wide range of ecological, social, and economic benefits beyond the production of food, fiber, and fuel. By recognizing and fostering multiple functions, agricultural systems can support biodiversity, maintain ecosystem services, enhance rural livelihoods, and contribute to climate resilience. This perspective shifts the focus from single-output, production-oriented models to holistic management that values the diverse roles agricultural land can play.

A multifunctional approach acknowledges that well-managed farms can regulate water flows, store carbon, promote soil formation, and support a variety of wildlife habitats. These benefits arise from integrating practices such as agroforestry, conservation tillage, cover cropping, and the maintenance of field margins and buffer strips. Such interventions not only sustain agricultural productivity but also improve water quality, prevent soil erosion, and create ecological corridors that enhance species movement across the landscape.

Social and cultural functions are also central to multifunctional agriculture. Farms often serve as spaces for recreation, education, and the preservation of cultural heritage. They support local economies through the creation of employment, the development of value-added products, and the maintenance of traditional knowledge and rural identity. By engaging communities and fostering stewardship, multifunctional agricultural systems contribute to social cohesion and well-being.

Economic diversification is another important aspect of multifunctionality. Integrating multiple enterprises—such as combining crop and livestock production, or incorporating agro-tourism—can increase farm income stability and provide buffers against market or environmental shocks. This diversified approach spreads risk and enhances the adaptive capacity of farming households and communities.

By designing agricultural systems with multifunctionality in mind, land managers can achieve synergies between productivity, environmental health, and social benefits. Such systems are better equipped to adapt to challenges, meet the needs of present and future generations, and contribute positively to broader sustainability goals. Multifunctionality represents a key principle of EBS, enabling agriculture to deliver a range of benefits that extend far beyond the farm gate.

Synergies Between Food Production and Environmental Stewardship

Synergies between food production and environmental stewardship highlight the potential for agriculture to meet human needs while actively supporting the health of ecosystems. Rather than viewing food production and environmental protection as competing objectives, EBS show that they can be mutually reinforcing. Well-designed agricultural systems can deliver abundant harvests and maintain or enhance soil, water, and biodiversity resources essential for long-term productivity.

Integrating ecological practices—such as crop diversification, conservation tillage, cover cropping, and agroforestry—enables farmers to reduce input use and environmental impact while improving yields and farm resilience. For example, incorporating trees and shrubs into farmland provides habitat for beneficial species, stabilizes soil, improves water retention, and supports pollination and pest regulation. These ecological benefits, in turn, enhance productivity and reduce the risk of crop failure.

Soil health lies at the heart of these synergies. Practices that protect and build soil organic matter, encourage microbial diversity, and minimize disturbance foster fertile, living soils capable of sustaining crops with fewer chemical inputs. Healthy soils store water more efficiently, buffer crops against drought, and cycle nutrients in ways that maintain long-term productivity and environmental integrity.

Water stewardship is another area where food production and ecosystem health align. Efficient irrigation, protection of riparian buffers, and the restoration of wetlands all support agricultural output while safeguarding water quality and aquatic biodiversity. Such measures help reduce runoff and pollution, enhance water infiltration, and maintain base flows in rivers and streams.

Farmers who embrace these synergies benefit from increased resilience, lower input costs, and greater access to ecosystem services—such as natural pest control and pollination—that are vital for productive agriculture. At the same time, landscapes managed with environmental stewardship in mind are better able to support wildlife, store carbon, and adapt to changing climate conditions.

By fostering these synergies, agricultural systems can be designed to thrive within environmental limits, contribute to sustainability goals, and ensure that food production goes hand in hand with the conservation of the natural resources upon which it depends.

Barriers To Adopting Ecosystem-Based Solutions

Despite the proven benefits of EBS in agriculture, a range of barriers can hinder their widespread adoption. One of the primary challenges is the persistence of conventional mindsets and the strong influence of established agricultural practices. Many farmers are accustomed to input-intensive approaches that prioritize short-term yields, making the transition to more holistic, ecosystem-oriented management unfamiliar or perceived as risky.

Economic constraints are another significant barrier. The initial costs associated with adopting new practices—such as purchasing cover crop seeds, establishing hedgerows, or investing in new equipment—can be prohibitive, especially for smallholders with limited access to credit. In many regions, markets and subsidies continue to favor conventional systems, reducing the financial incentives to shift toward EBS.

Knowledge gaps and limited access to information also impede adoption. Farmers may lack technical guidance on implementing ecosystem-based approaches or may be unaware of the long-term benefits these strategies can provide. Extension services, training programs, and peer-to-peer learning opportunities are often insufficient or unevenly distributed, leaving many producers without the support needed to make informed decisions.

Institutional and policy barriers further complicate the transition. Agricultural policies, land tenure systems, and regulatory frameworks may not be aligned with ecosystem-based principles, making it difficult to secure land for restoration or to receive recognition and rewards for ecosystem services. In some contexts, insecure land rights discourage investment in long-term sustainability measures.

Social and cultural factors can also influence the uptake of EBS. Traditional norms, risk aversion, and community perceptions may discourage experimentation or the adoption of unfamiliar practices. Successful implementation often requires collective action and coordination across farms and landscapes, which can be challenging to organize and sustain.

Finally, the impacts of climate change, market volatility, and resource scarcity can create uncertainty that makes farmers hesitant to alter their established systems. Overcoming these barriers involves addressing financial constraints, strengthening knowledge networks, adapting policies and institutions, and fostering a culture of innovation and collaboration. By creating enabling environments, stakeholders can help ensure that EBS become accessible, viable, and attractive options for farmers everywhere.

Chapter 2: Soil Health and Regenerative Practices

Chapter 2 delves into the pivotal role of soil health as the foundation of productive and resilient agricultural systems. Healthy soils are living ecosystems teeming with organisms that drive nutrient cycling, enhance water retention, and support plant growth. This chapter explores the principles of soil ecology and the importance of organic matter, biodiversity, and structure in maintaining long-term fertility. It examines regenerative practices—including conservation tillage, cover cropping, crop rotation, and organic amendments—that restore soil vitality while minimizing environmental impacts. By highlighting the connections between soil management and ecosystem services, this chapter demonstrates how investing in soil health not only sustains yields but also builds resilience to climate change and reduces dependency on external inputs. The discussion provides practical guidance for integrating regenerative approaches, setting the stage for a more sustainable, ecosystem-based model of agriculture.

Importance Of Soil as a Living Ecosystem

Soil is far more than just a medium for plant roots; it is a dynamic, living ecosystem teeming with microorganisms, fungi, insects, earthworms, and countless other organisms. This complex web of life is fundamental to the health and productivity of agricultural systems. Healthy soils perform essential ecosystem functions, including nutrient cycling, water filtration, carbon storage, and the suppression of pests and diseases. Recognizing and managing soil as a living ecosystem is at the heart of sustainable and resilient agriculture.

At the microscopic level, bacteria and fungi break down organic matter, releasing nutrients in forms that plants can absorb. These organisms also form symbiotic relationships with plant roots, enhancing nutrient uptake and improving plant health. Earthworms and other soil fauna aerate the soil, improve structure, and further contribute to the decomposition of organic material. Collectively, these processes maintain soil fertility and structure, creating an environment where crops can thrive with reduced need for external inputs.

Healthy soils store and regulate water, making them more resilient to drought and heavy rainfall. The presence of organic matter increases the soil's capacity to retain moisture and prevents erosion by binding soil particles together. This not only supports consistent crop growth but also protects downstream water quality by reducing sediment and nutrient runoff.

Soil biodiversity underpins the resilience of agricultural systems. Diverse communities of organisms help buffer crops against pest outbreaks and disease, while also supporting the natural breakdown of pollutants and contaminants. The loss of soil life—due to overuse of chemicals, compaction, or erosion—leads to declining soil health, reduced productivity, and increased vulnerability to environmental stresses.

Managing soil as a living ecosystem involves practices that protect and enhance soil life, such as minimizing tillage, maintaining organic cover, rotating crops, and applying organic amendments. These strategies foster a vibrant soil community, reduce reliance on synthetic fertilizers and pesticides, and build the foundation for long-term agricultural sustainability. By valuing the living nature of soil, farmers and land managers ensure that their fields remain productive, resilient, and capable of supporting future generations.

Enhancing Soil Organic Matter

Soil organic matter is a cornerstone of soil health and fertility, playing a vital role in maintaining productive and resilient agricultural systems. Composed of decomposing plant and animal residues, microorganisms, and stable humus, organic matter improves soil structure, water retention, nutrient availability, and biological activity. Enhancing soil organic matter is essential for supporting the wide range of ecosystem services upon which successful farming depends.

Incorporating organic matter into soils begins with practices that return plant residues, such as crop stubble and green manures, directly to the field. Cover crops, when grown between main crops, not only protect the soil from erosion but also add organic material when incorporated back into the soil. Rotating crops with legumes or other species that fix atmospheric nitrogen further enriches organic content and boosts soil fertility.

Adding compost, animal manures, or other organic amendments increases the organic content and stimulates microbial activity. These additions supply nutrients slowly, reducing the need for synthetic fertilizers and creating a more balanced soil ecosystem. As microorganisms break down organic materials, they release nutrients in plant-available forms while also producing substances that help bind soil particles, improving structure and aeration.

Conservation tillage, or reduced tillage, helps to preserve soil organic matter by minimizing disturbance and preventing rapid decomposition and loss of carbon to the atmosphere. Maintaining permanent or semi-permanent vegetation cover, such as with perennial crops or agroforestry, further contributes to organic matter accumulation over time.

Enhancing soil organic matter also boosts soil's capacity to retain moisture, buffer pH, and support beneficial soil organisms, creating a more resilient environment for crops. This, in turn, reduces vulnerability to drought, heavy rainfall, and pest pressures. Healthy soils rich in organic matter are less prone to erosion and can sequester significant amounts of carbon, supporting climate mitigation goals.

A long-term commitment to building soil organic matter delivers lasting benefits for both agriculture and the environment. By integrating a combination of residue management, organic amendments, crop rotation, and conservation tillage, farmers can sustain productive soils and foster EBS that underpin the health and resilience of agricultural landscapes.

Conservation Tillage and No-Till Farming

Conservation tillage and no-till farming are pivotal practices in ecosystem-based agriculture, designed to minimize soil disturbance and protect the living structure of soils. Unlike conventional plowing, which turns over the soil and disrupts soil life, these approaches leave crop residues on the surface and reduce or eliminate mechanical soil inversion. The result is improved soil health, greater resilience, and a suite of benefits for both the farm and the wider environment.

In conservation tillage systems, at least 30% of the soil surface remains covered with crop residues after planting. This protective layer helps shield the soil from erosion by wind and water, preserves moisture, and moderates temperature fluctuations. Crop residues also provide food and habitat for earthworms, insects, and microorganisms, which are vital for nutrient cycling and soil structure.

No-till farming goes further by planting seeds directly into undisturbed soil. This method fosters the accumulation of organic matter, improves soil aggregation, and allows roots to penetrate deeply, enhancing the soil's capacity to absorb and retain water. No-till systems often require the use of specialized seeding equipment to manage residue cover while ensuring proper seed placement.

Both conservation tillage and no-till farming reduce the loss of soil carbon and enhance the soil's potential to sequester atmospheric carbon, supporting climate change mitigation efforts. By minimizing disturbance, these practices help maintain the integrity of soil food webs and support beneficial soil organisms, including mycorrhizal fungi that improve plant nutrient uptake.

Adopting these approaches also lowers fuel and labor requirements, as fewer field passes are needed. Over time, reduced tillage can decrease the incidence of soil compaction and reduce the energy costs of farming. However, these systems may require new weed management strategies and a period of adjustment as soil structure and biological communities recover from previous intensive tillage.

By maintaining soil cover, enhancing organic matter, and reducing disturbance, conservation tillage and no-till farming provide foundational benefits for ecosystem-based agriculture. These practices foster healthier, more resilient soils, support long-term productivity, and contribute to the sustainability of agricultural landscapes.

Cover Cropping and Green Manures

Cover cropping and the use of green manures are integral practices in ecosystem-based agriculture, contributing to soil health, fertility, and overall farm resilience. Cover crops are non-harvested plants grown between periods of regular crop production. Green manures are cover crops that are specifically incorporated into the soil to add organic matter and nutrients. Both approaches play a vital role in maintaining and improving soil quality, enhancing ecosystem functions, and supporting sustainable agricultural systems.

The main functions of cover crops include protecting the soil from erosion, suppressing weeds, enhancing soil structure, and promoting water infiltration. Species selection is tailored to specific goals— legumes such as clover and vetch fix atmospheric nitrogen, enriching soil fertility, while grasses like rye and oats build biomass and scavenge residual nutrients. The diversity of cover crop species can also help break pest and disease cycles by interrupting the continuous presence of host plants.

Green manures are managed so that they are incorporated into the soil while still green and succulent, providing a rapid infusion of organic matter and nutrients. This process stimulates soil microbial activity, increases the availability of plant nutrients, and improves soil tilth. As the green manure decomposes, it releases nitrogen and other nutrients in forms that are readily available to subsequent crops, reducing the need for synthetic fertilizers.

Both cover cropping and green manuring help build soil organic matter, which improves soil structure, water retention, and resilience to extreme weather. The living roots of cover crops stabilize soil, reduce compaction, and create channels for air and water movement. Their residues enhance the habitat for earthworms and other beneficial organisms, strengthening the soil food web.

Implementing cover cropping and green manures requires careful planning regarding species choice, timing of planting and incorporation, and integration into existing crop rotations. With appropriate management, these practices can deliver long-term gains in soil health and productivity, reduce input costs, and foster the ecological balance necessary for resilient agricultural systems. By supporting the natural functions of the soil ecosystem, cover crops and green manures are foundational tools for advancing EBS in agriculture.

Crop Rotation and Diversification

Crop rotation and diversification are essential strategies in ecosystem-based agriculture, supporting soil health, pest management, and sustainable productivity. Crop rotation involves the planned sequence of different crops on the same field across seasons or years, rather than repeatedly planting the same crop. Diversification extends beyond rotation to include the integration of multiple crop species and varieties, sometimes along with livestock or agroforestry elements, within the farming system.

Rotating crops disrupts the life cycles of pests and diseases by breaking the continuous availability of their preferred host plants. For example, planting legumes after cereals helps to naturally reduce populations of soil-borne pathogens and pests specific to each crop, lowering the reliance on chemical pesticides. In addition, different crops have varying nutrient requirements and rooting depths, which helps to balance soil fertility and reduce nutrient depletion.

Diversification brings additional benefits. Growing a mix of species and varieties enhances resilience by spreading risk—if one crop fails due to pests, disease, or weather extremes, others can still provide yield and income. Incorporating cover crops, legumes, or deep-rooted plants increases organic matter input, promotes beneficial soil microbes, and helps cycle nutrients within the system. Mixed cropping and polycultures create more complex habitats that support pollinators and natural enemies of pests, contributing to ecological balance.

The integration of livestock or agroforestry adds further diversity, recycling nutrients through manure, providing additional products, and strengthening the overall resilience of the system. These integrated approaches help buffer farms against market fluctuations, weather extremes, and changing environmental conditions.

Planning effective crop rotations and diversification requires knowledge of local conditions, market demands, and the ecological interactions among crops. Successful implementation involves mapping out rotation sequences, monitoring soil health, and adjusting practices based on experience and observation. Farmers benefit from improved soil structure, reduced weed pressure, and more stable yields over time.

By fostering diversity above and below ground, crop rotation and diversification create robust agricultural systems that are less vulnerable to shocks, more productive in the long term, and aligned with the principles of EBS. These approaches lay the groundwork for regenerative, sustainable farming landscapes.

Managing Soil Biodiversity

Managing soil biodiversity is a crucial element of ecosystem-based agriculture, as the abundance and diversity of soil organisms underpin nearly every function essential to productive and resilient farming. Soil is home to a vast array of life forms—including bacteria, fungi, protozoa, nematodes, arthropods, and earthworms—each playing specialized roles in decomposition, nutrient cycling, soil structure formation, and plant health. Recognizing the value of this hidden biodiversity allows farmers to develop practices that protect and enhance the living soil community.

Soil microorganisms, such as bacteria and fungi, are responsible for breaking down organic matter, making nutrients available to plants, and suppressing soil-borne diseases. Mycorrhizal fungi form symbiotic associations with plant roots, improving water and nutrient uptake while increasing resistance to stress and disease. Larger soil fauna, including earthworms and arthropods, physically mix and aerate the soil, create channels for root growth and water infiltration, and further fragment organic residues.

Promoting soil biodiversity begins with minimizing soil disturbance through reduced or no-till farming. Maintaining continuous organic cover—whether through cover crops, crop residues, or mulches—provides food and habitat for soil organisms, helping them thrive year-round. Diversifying crop rotations supports a wide range of microbial and faunal communities, as different plants exude different root compounds that feed specific soil biota.

Avoiding overuse of synthetic chemicals, such as pesticides and fertilizers, is another key step. Excessive inputs can harm beneficial organisms, disrupt natural balances, and lead to declines in soil biodiversity. Instead, integrating organic amendments like compost, manure, and green manures supports microbial activity and builds resilient soil communities.

Water management also influences soil biodiversity, as both excessive and insufficient moisture can stress soil life. Good drainage, mulching, and practices that build soil structure help regulate soil moisture and create stable habitats for soil organisms.

By managing for soil biodiversity, farmers gain multiple benefits: improved nutrient cycling, greater disease and pest suppression, enhanced soil structure, and increased resilience to environmental stress. These outcomes form the foundation of EBS in agriculture, contributing to both sustainable productivity and long-term environmental health.

Soil Erosion Control Strategies

Soil erosion control is essential for maintaining long-term productivity and sustainability in agricultural landscapes. Erosion, caused by wind, water, or tillage, leads to the loss of fertile topsoil, reduced soil depth, diminished nutrient reserves, and impaired water-holding capacity. Effective control strategies focus on preserving soil cover, improving structure, and minimizing forces that dislodge or transport soil particles.

Maintaining continuous ground cover is one of the most effective defenses against erosion. Growing cover crops during fallow periods, leaving crop residues on the surface, or maintaining perennial vegetation helps protect the soil from raindrop impact and wind. These practices slow water runoff, allowing more time for infiltration and reducing the risk of soil particles being washed away. Mulching, using either organic or synthetic materials, also shields the soil from direct exposure and maintains moisture.

Contour farming and strip cropping are important landscape-level strategies. Planting along natural land contours slows the flow of water and reduces its erosive power. Strip cropping alternates rows of erosion-prone crops with strips of dense vegetation, such as grass or legumes, to intercept runoff and trap sediments. Terracing, which involves reshaping steep slopes into a series of level steps, is highly effective in mountainous or hilly regions, greatly reducing water movement and soil loss.

Wind erosion can be minimized by establishing windbreaks or shelterbelts—rows of trees or shrubs that reduce wind speed and protect fields. Maintaining soil moisture through irrigation or conservation tillage further reduces the risk of wind-blown soil.

Soil structure is fundamental to erosion control. Practices that increase organic matter, such as applying compost or manure and minimizing tillage, help bind soil particles together and improve aggregation. Well-structured soils absorb water more efficiently, reducing surface runoff and erosion risk.

Buffer strips of vegetation along waterways act as filters, trapping sediments and preventing soil from entering streams or rivers. These areas also provide habitat for beneficial wildlife and help maintain water quality.

Implementing a combination of these strategies, tailored to site-specific conditions, enables farmers to preserve their most valuable resource—the soil. By controlling erosion, agricultural systems become more resilient, maintain higher yields, and support broader ecosystem health for future generations.

Chapter 3: Water Management for Resilient Agriculture

Chapter 3 focuses on the central role of water management in building resilient agricultural systems. Water is fundamental to crop growth, soil health, and ecosystem function, yet its availability and quality are increasingly threatened by climate change, overuse, and pollution. This chapter examines the hydrological cycle within agricultural landscapes and the impacts of different farming practices on water resources. It explores ecosystem-based approaches to irrigation, on-farm water harvesting, wetland integration, and drought management that work in harmony with natural processes. By emphasizing efficient, adaptive, and environmentally conscious water use, the discussion highlights strategies that enhance productivity while safeguarding water supplies for future generations. The chapter equips readers with practical insights for integrating water conservation and resilience into everyday agricultural management.

The Hydrological Cycle in Agricultural Systems

The hydrological cycle, or water cycle, is a continuous process that moves water through the environment, underpinning the productivity and resilience of agricultural systems. In farming landscapes, water is absorbed by plant roots from the soil, transpires through leaves, evaporates from land and water surfaces, and returns to the ground as precipitation. Understanding how water moves within agricultural settings is crucial for managing both crop production and ecosystem health.

Rainfall or irrigation supplies water to fields, where it infiltrates the soil and becomes available to plants. Some water is stored in the soil profile, supporting crops during dry periods, while excess water may percolate deeper to recharge groundwater or run off the surface into nearby streams, rivers, or reservoirs. The rate and amount of infiltration depend on soil type, structure, organic matter, and land management practices. Well-structured soils with high organic content absorb and retain more water, reducing runoff and erosion.

Transpiration, the process by which plants release water vapor through their leaves, is a key component of the cycle in agricultural landscapes. Alongside evaporation from soil and water surfaces, transpiration returns significant amounts of water to the atmosphere. This combined process, known as evapotranspiration, is influenced by weather conditions, crop type, and stage of growth.

Agricultural practices can profoundly affect the hydrological cycle. Intensive tillage, removal of vegetation, and overgrazing reduce infiltration, increase runoff, and elevate the risk of soil erosion and nutrient loss. Conversely, practices such as cover cropping, conservation tillage, and the use of buffer strips help maintain soil structure, promote water retention, and moderate the flow of water across fields.

Effective water management in agriculture seeks to align farming activities with the natural hydrological cycle. By capturing rainfall, minimizing losses, and improving water use efficiency, farmers can enhance both productivity and environmental sustainability. A deep understanding of the hydrological cycle allows for informed decisions on irrigation scheduling, drainage, and landscape design, ensuring that water resources are used wisely and conserved for future generations.

Ecosystem-Based Irrigation Management

Ecosystem-based irrigation management focuses on aligning irrigation practices with natural processes to optimize water use, maintain soil health, and protect surrounding ecosystems. Rather than simply delivering water to crops on a set schedule, this approach considers soil moisture dynamics, plant needs, weather patterns, and the broader landscape context. It aims to balance crop productivity with resource efficiency and long-term sustainability.

The first principle of ecosystem-based irrigation management is understanding the specific water requirements of different crops at various growth stages. By tailoring irrigation to crop demand, farmers can avoid overwatering, which wastes water and can lead to nutrient leaching, root diseases, and reduced soil aeration. Soil moisture monitoring—using sensors, tensiometers, or simple field observations—enables more precise application of water, matching supply with actual plant needs.

Selecting appropriate irrigation methods is another critical aspect. Drip and micro-irrigation systems deliver water directly to plant roots, minimizing evaporation losses and runoff. These systems are especially effective in conserving water and maintaining optimal soil moisture levels. When surface or sprinkler irrigation is used, scheduling and application rates should be carefully managed to prevent excess runoff and soil compaction.

Integrating landscape features, such as contour bunds, swales, and retention ponds, helps capture and store rainfall, recharge groundwater, and slow surface water movement. Maintaining healthy soils with high organic matter content increases water infiltration and retention, reducing the need for frequent irrigation and building resilience to drought.

Ecosystem-based management also accounts for the potential impacts of irrigation on surrounding environments. Buffer strips along waterways, protection of wetlands, and careful management of return flows help prevent pollution and protect aquatic habitats. Rotating irrigated crops with dryland or cover crops can give soils time to recover and further reduce water demand.

By combining efficient technology, adaptive scheduling, and ecological principles, ecosystem-based irrigation management maximizes the benefits of each drop of water. This approach reduces input costs, supports healthier crops, and safeguards the natural systems that agriculture depends on. In doing so, it fosters both high yields and sustainable resource use, securing water supplies for farms and communities into the future.

On-Farm Water Harvesting Techniques

On-farm water harvesting techniques are vital components of ecosystem-based agriculture, enabling farmers to capture, store, and efficiently utilize rainfall and surface water. These methods increase water availability during dry periods, enhance resilience to drought, and reduce reliance on external water sources. By working with the landscape and hydrological cycle, water harvesting supports both crop production and ecosystem health.

One widely used technique is the construction of farm ponds and reservoirs to collect rainwater runoff from fields, rooftops, and other surfaces. These storage systems can be lined or unlined, and their capacity is designed to meet irrigation and livestock needs during dry spells. Ponds also contribute to groundwater recharge by allowing some of the stored water to percolate into the soil.

Contour bunding and terracing are landscape modifications that slow and direct surface runoff, increasing water infiltration and reducing erosion. Bunds—embankments built along the contour lines of a slope—trap rainwater and prevent it from quickly flowing off the land. Terraces convert steep slopes into a series of flat, step-like fields, enabling more effective water capture and reducing soil loss.

Check dams and small weirs built across streams or drainage channels temporarily hold back water, increasing infiltration and sediment deposition. These structures are particularly useful in areas with seasonal rainfall, as they retain water that would otherwise be lost as runoff. They also help restore local water tables and support downstream ecosystems.

Rainwater harvesting from roofs involves collecting precipitation from building surfaces and channeling it into tanks or underground cisterns. This approach provides a source of clean water for household use, irrigation, or livestock, and reduces demand on community water supplies.

Vegetative measures, such as planting grass strips, shelterbelts, or agroforestry systems, further enhance water harvesting by improving soil structure, reducing runoff velocity, and increasing infiltration. These practices integrate water conservation with habitat creation and soil health improvement.

By combining physical structures with vegetative strategies, on-farm water harvesting techniques make the most of available rainfall and help stabilize water supplies. These approaches build resilience, support sustainable production, and are central to EBS for managing agricultural water resources.

Buffer Strips and Riparian Zones

Buffer strips and riparian zones are essential features in ecosystem-based agricultural landscapes, serving as protective barriers between cultivated fields and water bodies. These vegetated areas play a critical role in safeguarding water quality, controlling erosion, supporting biodiversity, and enhancing the overall resilience of agricultural systems.

Buffer strips are typically bands of grass, shrubs, or trees established along field edges, waterways, or drainage ditches. Their dense vegetation acts as a filter, trapping sediments, nutrients, and pesticides before they can enter streams, rivers, or lakes. This interception reduces the risk of water pollution, protects aquatic ecosystems, and maintains the quality of downstream water supplies. Buffer strips also help slow surface runoff, allowing more time for water to infiltrate the soil, thereby reducing erosion and flooding risk.

Riparian zones refer to the natural or managed areas adjacent to rivers, streams, and other watercourses. These zones are characterized by moisture-loving plants, including native grasses, shrubs, and trees, which stabilize stream banks and create habitat for a wide array of wildlife. Healthy riparian zones support amphibians, birds, insects, and aquatic species, contributing to landscape connectivity and ecological balance.

In addition to their water quality and habitat benefits, buffer strips and riparian zones moderate local microclimates, provide shade to water bodies (helping regulate temperature for aquatic life), and act as corridors for the movement of species. Their deep-rooted vegetation improves soil structure, enhances carbon sequestration, and increases resilience to extreme weather events.

Implementing buffer strips and restoring or conserving riparian zones require careful planning regarding width, plant species selection, and management practices. Wider buffers and a mix of native plants generally offer greater environmental benefits. Regular maintenance—such as controlling invasive species and periodic mowing or thinning—ensures these areas remain effective over time.

By incorporating buffer strips and riparian zones into farm planning, agricultural producers can achieve multiple objectives: protecting natural resources, supporting biodiversity, and sustaining productive land. These practices exemplify the synergies possible between food production and environmental stewardship in ecosystem-based agricultural systems.

Wetland Integration for Water Purification

Wetlands are natural water purifiers, and their integration into agricultural landscapes is a powerful ecosystem-based solution for enhancing water quality and ecological health. Wetlands—whether natural, restored, or constructed—act as biofilters that remove sediments, nutrients, pesticides, and other contaminants from surface runoff and drainage water before it enters rivers, streams, or groundwater systems. This process helps protect both local water supplies and downstream ecosystems.

Wetlands achieve purification through a combination of physical, chemical, and biological processes. As water flows slowly through wetland vegetation, sediments settle out, and pollutants are trapped or absorbed by plants and soil. Wetland plants, such as reeds, sedges, and rushes, take up excess nutrients like nitrogen and phosphorus, reducing the risk of eutrophication in water bodies. Microbial activity in the saturated soils breaks down organic matter and transforms harmful substances into less toxic forms, further improving water quality.

Constructed wetlands are specifically designed and engineered to treat agricultural runoff and drainage. These systems mimic the functions of natural wetlands but are integrated into farm layouts to intercept water at strategic points, such as field edges or drainage outlets. Constructed wetlands are cost-effective, require low maintenance, and provide multiple benefits, including wildlife habitat and aesthetic value.

Restoring degraded natural wetlands within or near farmlands can also yield significant purification benefits. Wetland restoration involves reestablishing hydrology, replanting native vegetation, and removing barriers to natural water flow. This not only improves water quality but also enhances flood control, groundwater recharge, and landscape biodiversity.

Wetland integration requires careful siting, design, and management to maximize effectiveness. The size, depth, vegetation type, and water flow must be tailored to local conditions and intended functions. Ongoing maintenance, such as managing plant growth and removing accumulated sediments, ensures long-term performance.

By incorporating wetlands into agricultural systems, farmers and land managers can reduce pollution, meet regulatory requirements, and foster healthier ecosystems. Wetlands contribute to the resilience and sustainability of agricultural landscapes, supporting both productive farming and the conservation of vital water resources.

Managing Water Scarcity And Drought

Managing water scarcity and drought is a central challenge for sustainable agriculture, especially as climate variability and competition for water resources intensify. Ecosystem-based approaches offer a suite of strategies to help farms adapt to limited water availability, maintain productivity, and reduce vulnerability to prolonged dry periods.

Efficient irrigation management is foundational to coping with scarcity. This includes adopting water-saving technologies such as drip or micro-irrigation, which deliver water directly to plant roots with minimal losses from evaporation or runoff. Scheduling irrigation based on actual soil moisture and crop needs, rather than fixed calendars, ensures water is applied only when necessary. Soil moisture sensors and weather-based decision tools support precision in water use.

Building soil health is another key strategy. Practices that increase soil organic matter—such as cover cropping, reduced tillage, and organic amendments—improve soil structure and enhance the soil's ability to absorb and store water. Healthy soils retain moisture longer, buffering crops against drought stress and reducing irrigation requirements.

Landscape-level interventions also play a role in managing water scarcity. On-farm water harvesting structures, like ponds, swales, and contour bunds, capture and store rainfall for use during dry spells. Planting shelterbelts and agroforestry systems reduces evaporation and wind erosion, while deep-rooted perennial plants access water from deeper soil layers.

Crop selection and diversification further strengthen resilience. Choosing drought-tolerant crop varieties, rotating crops to balance water demand, and integrating livestock can spread risk and stabilize yields under changing conditions. Shorter-season crops or adjusting planting dates can help avoid peak drought periods.

Engaging with community-based water management initiatives allows farmers to coordinate withdrawals, share resources, and participate in collective planning for drought preparedness. Policy support and access to information, financial incentives, and technical assistance all contribute to building adaptive capacity.

By integrating these ecosystem-based strategies, farmers can optimize limited water supplies, protect crops, and sustain production even in challenging conditions. Managing water scarcity and drought through ecological principles not only reduces risk but also supports the long-term viability and resilience of agricultural systems in the face of an uncertain climate future.

Reducing Agricultural Water Pollution

Reducing agricultural water pollution is vital for protecting both environmental and human health. Ecosystem-based approaches focus on preventing contaminants—such as nutrients, sediments, pesticides, and pathogens—from leaving farm fields and entering rivers, lakes, and groundwater. By integrating ecological principles and best management practices, agriculture can minimize its impact on water quality while maintaining productive systems.

Nutrient management is a primary strategy. Applying fertilizers and manure at the right rate, time, and place ensures that crops absorb nutrients efficiently, reducing the risk of excess nitrogen and phosphorus leaching into waterways. Regular soil testing, split fertilizer applications, and precision agriculture technologies help farmers match nutrient supply to crop demand and avoid over-application. Cover crops and deep-rooted plants further capture residual nutrients, preventing them from washing away with rain or irrigation.

Erosion control plays a key role in reducing sediment runoff, which often carries attached nutrients and pesticides into water bodies. Maintaining ground cover, practicing conservation tillage, and planting buffer strips along field edges and waterways stabilize soil, trap sediments, and intercept pollutants before they reach aquatic systems.

IPM reduces reliance on chemical pesticides by emphasizing crop rotations, biological controls, and habitat enhancement for natural pest enemies. When pesticides are necessary, choosing targeted products and applying them only when and where needed minimizes off-target movement and contamination risks.

Constructed wetlands, retention ponds, and vegetated drainage ditches can intercept and treat runoff before it leaves the farm. These landscape features filter sediments and nutrients, while the plants and microorganisms break down and absorb pollutants.

Managing livestock access to streams and water bodies is also important. Fencing off riparian areas, providing alternative watering points, and managing manure storage reduce direct nutrient and pathogen loading to watercourses.

Engagement with watershed-level initiatives and compliance with regulations further strengthen efforts to protect water quality. Farmers can benefit from education, technical assistance, and incentives that support the adoption of pollution-reducing practices.

By implementing a combination of field-level and landscape-scale measures, agricultural producers can dramatically reduce water pollution. These actions not only safeguard vital water resources but also build the foundation for resilient, sustainable farming systems that benefit both people and nature.

Chapter 4: Enhancing Biodiversity in Farmland

Chapter 4 explores the vital importance of biodiversity in creating healthy, productive, and resilient farmland. Biodiversity underpins the ecological functions that sustain agriculture, including pollination, pest regulation, nutrient cycling, and soil health. This chapter examines how diverse plant and animal life within and around fields enhances ecosystem services, stabilizes yields, and buffers farms against environmental shocks. It discusses practical strategies for habitat creation and restoration, integrating trees and agroforestry, managing field margins, and supporting pollinators and natural enemies of pests. By weaving biodiversity into the fabric of agricultural landscapes, farmers can reduce reliance on chemical inputs, strengthen ecological resilience, and support broader conservation goals. The chapter provides a roadmap for fostering biodiversity through EBS, making the case for its central role in sustainable farming systems.

Biodiversity as a Foundation of Ecosystem Function

Biodiversity forms the foundation of ecosystem function in agricultural landscapes, underpinning the services that sustain productivity, resilience, and environmental health. A diverse array of plants, animals, microorganisms, and genetic resources interact within these systems, shaping soil fertility, water regulation, pest control, and pollination. When agricultural landscapes support rich biodiversity, they are better equipped to adapt to change, recover from disturbances, and maintain critical ecological processes.

The presence of multiple plant species in fields, hedgerows, and non-cropped areas increases the variety of habitats and food sources available for beneficial insects, birds, and other wildlife. This diversity attracts natural enemies of pests, reduces outbreaks, and helps maintain ecological balance. Genetic diversity within crops and livestock enhances adaptability to disease, climate stress, and changing market demands, reducing the risks associated with monocultures.

Soil biodiversity is equally crucial. A complex web of bacteria, fungi, earthworms, and other organisms drives nutrient cycling, organic matter decomposition, and soil structure formation. Healthy, biodiverse soils can buffer crops against drought and disease, absorb and filter water more effectively, and store more carbon, supporting both productivity and environmental goals.

Biodiversity also stabilizes agricultural ecosystems by providing ecological redundancy—different species often fulfill similar roles, ensuring that key functions persist even if some species decline. This resilience is vital as farms face the challenges of climate variability, pest invasions, and shifting growing conditions.

Practices such as crop rotation, intercropping, maintaining wild margins, and restoring native vegetation all help foster biodiversity on farms. Minimizing chemical use, reducing disturbance, and creating habitat corridors further support the diversity of life in agricultural landscapes.

By prioritizing biodiversity, farmers and land managers enhance the delivery of ecosystem services that are fundamental to agricultural success. The result is a more robust and sustainable system, capable of producing food while conserving the natural resources on which farming depends. Biodiversity is not only a resource to be preserved but an active force that drives the health and function of agricultural ecosystems.

Habitat Creation and Restoration In Agricultural Settings

Habitat creation and restoration within agricultural landscapes are essential strategies for enhancing biodiversity and strengthening ecosystem functions. As agricultural expansion and intensification have often led to habitat loss and fragmentation, actively restoring and creating diverse habitats helps to reverse these trends, providing essential refuges for wildlife and supporting the ecological processes that underpin productive farming.

Creating habitats begins with setting aside portions of farmland for non-cropped features, such as native grasslands, wildflower strips, woodlots, and ponds. These areas serve as sanctuaries for pollinators, birds, beneficial insects, and other wildlife that contribute to pest control, pollination, and nutrient cycling. Establishing hedgerows or shelterbelts along field boundaries offers food, shelter, and corridors for species movement, enhancing landscape connectivity and resilience.

Restoring degraded habitats involves re-establishing natural vegetation, improving soil health, and reinstating natural hydrological regimes. For example, planting native species in previously cleared or eroded areas, rewetting drained wetlands, and stabilizing stream banks with riparian vegetation all help return ecological integrity to agricultural settings. Restoration also means removing invasive species and barriers to wildlife movement, allowing native plants and animals to recolonize and thrive.

Incorporating habitat creation and restoration into farm management delivers multiple benefits. Enhanced biodiversity increases natural pest control, supports pollinator populations, and improves soil and water quality. Diverse habitats also buffer agricultural systems against environmental shocks, such as floods, droughts, and disease outbreaks, by supporting a wider range of species and ecosystem functions.

Planning and maintaining habitats require understanding local ecological conditions, selecting appropriate plant species, and integrating habitats into existing land uses without compromising production. In many cases, even small habitat features can yield significant gains for biodiversity and ecosystem services.

By committing to habitat creation and restoration, farmers help sustain the ecological foundation of agriculture, contributing to productive, resilient, and sustainable food systems. These efforts support not only wildlife and ecosystem health but also the long-term viability of farming communities and the landscapes they steward.

Hedgerows, Field Margins, and Shelterbelts

Hedgerows, field margins, and shelterbelts are important linear features in agricultural landscapes that deliver multiple ecological and production benefits. These vegetated strips—composed of trees, shrubs, grasses, or a mix of species—are typically established along field edges, boundaries, or within the interior of large fields. They serve as vital habitats for wildlife, improve farm microclimates, and contribute to the resilience and sustainability of agricultural systems.

Hedgerows are dense rows of shrubs or small trees planted along the edges of fields or roads. They provide food, shelter, and corridors for a variety of species, including pollinators, birds, and natural enemies of crop pests. By increasing habitat complexity and connectivity, hedgerows enhance biodiversity and promote the presence of beneficial organisms that support natural pest regulation and pollination.

Field margins are uncultivated strips left alongside the edges of cropped fields. These areas often contain native grasses and wildflowers, offering resources for pollinators, insects, and small mammals. Field margins act as buffer zones that filter runoff, trap sediments, and reduce the movement of pesticides and nutrients into adjacent waterways, helping to protect water quality.

Shelterbelts, or windbreaks, are rows of trees or tall shrubs planted at intervals across fields to reduce wind speed and provide shelter. By moderating wind, shelterbelts help prevent soil erosion, reduce evapotranspiration, and protect crops from wind damage. They also create microclimates that can improve crop growth, increase moisture retention, and extend the growing season.

Together, these features support landscape connectivity, enabling wildlife to move safely between habitats and maintain viable populations. They contribute to ecological resilience by supporting a diversity of species and functions, while also providing practical benefits such as reduced input costs, enhanced pollination, and improved soil and water conservation.

The successful establishment and management of hedgerows, field margins, and shelterbelts require thoughtful planning, including the selection of appropriate native species, ongoing maintenance, and integration into farm operations. By incorporating these linear habitats, farmers strengthen the ecological infrastructure of their land and foster multifunctional landscapes that benefit both agriculture and the environment.

Integrating Trees and Agroforestry

Integrating trees into agricultural systems through agroforestry offers a powerful way to enhance biodiversity, improve soil health, and boost farm resilience. Agroforestry involves the intentional incorporation of trees and shrubs with crops and/or livestock on the same land, creating diverse and multifunctional landscapes. This practice draws on ecological principles, harnessing the complementary relationships between trees, crops, and animals to optimize productivity and sustainability.

Trees in agroforestry systems provide numerous ecosystem services. Their roots stabilize soil, reduce erosion, and increase infiltration, while leaf litter adds organic matter, enhancing soil fertility and structure. Deep-rooted trees access nutrients and water from lower soil layers, recycling them to the surface for use by crops and pasture plants. The shade provided by trees moderates microclimates, reducing heat and moisture stress on crops and livestock.

Agroforestry systems also support a wide range of wildlife by creating habitat diversity and corridors for movement. Birds, insects, and mammals benefit from food, shelter, and breeding sites, which in turn supports natural pest control and pollination. In addition, trees sequester carbon, contribute to climate change mitigation, and help regulate local water cycles.

Several types of agroforestry can be tailored to different farming contexts. Alley cropping integrates rows of trees within crops, silvopasture combines trees with grazing livestock, and windbreaks use trees to protect fields from wind and erosion. Multi-strata systems—such as home gardens and forest gardens—layer different plant types, maximizing productivity and resilience.

Successful integration of trees and agroforestry requires careful planning regarding tree species selection, spacing, and compatibility with crops or livestock. Management practices should address competition for light, water, and nutrients, as well as the timing of pruning and harvesting to maintain system balance.

By adopting agroforestry, farmers diversify their sources of income and products—such as fruit, timber, fodder, and fuelwood—while strengthening the underlying health and sustainability of their land. Integrating trees into agricultural systems exemplifies the principles of EBS, building landscapes that are productive, ecologically robust, and adaptable to future challenges.

Pollinator Support and Management

Pollinator support and management are central to sustaining agricultural productivity and ecosystem health. Pollinators—including bees, butterflies, moths, beetles, and other insects, as well as birds and bats—are responsible for the fertilization of many crops and wild plants, enabling fruit and seed production. In agricultural systems, effective pollination leads to higher yields, improved crop quality, and greater resilience to environmental stresses.

A decline in pollinator populations, driven by habitat loss, pesticide exposure, disease, and climate change, poses a significant threat to food security. To address this, farms can adopt a range of ecosystem-based practices that foster healthy pollinator communities and create supportive environments for their survival and reproduction.

Habitat provision is a primary strategy. Establishing wildflower strips, flowering cover crops, hedgerows, and uncultivated field margins offers foraging resources and nesting sites for pollinators throughout the growing season. Selecting a diversity of native plant species ensures blooms are available at different times, supporting a wide variety of pollinator species and life cycles.

Reducing the use of harmful pesticides, especially those known to be toxic to pollinators, is another crucial step. IPM techniques prioritize biological and cultural controls, applying chemical products only as a last resort and targeting them precisely to minimize risks to non-target organisms.

Preserving natural habitats, such as woodlots, wetlands, and undisturbed patches, provides essential refuges for pollinators during periods of disturbance or scarcity. Providing water sources, bare ground, and nesting substrates further enhances the suitability of agricultural landscapes for both managed and wild pollinators.

Education and collaboration among farmers, beekeepers, and communities support the adoption of best practices and the early detection of pollinator health issues. Monitoring pollinator populations and assessing their effectiveness helps guide adaptive management and ensures that conservation efforts are effective.

By actively supporting and managing pollinator communities, farms secure the ecosystem services needed for sustainable production and biodiversity conservation. These actions build agricultural systems that are both productive and resilient, benefiting farmers, consumers, and the wider environment.

Functional Diversity and Pest Regulation

Functional diversity—the range of different biological roles performed by organisms in a system—is a key driver of pest regulation in agricultural landscapes. Rather than relying on single-species solutions or chemical controls, ecosystem-based agriculture harnesses the interactions among a variety of plants, animals, and microorganisms to suppress pest populations and maintain ecological balance.

Different plant species in a diverse cropping system support various beneficial insects, such as predators and parasitoids, which feed on or disrupt the life cycles of crop pests. For example, flowering plants attract hoverflies, lacewings, and lady beetles, all of which prey on aphids and other harmful insects. By providing continuous sources of nectar, pollen, and alternative prey, diversified plantings ensure these beneficial populations are sustained throughout the growing season.

Ground cover and vegetation structure are equally important. Mulches, cover crops, and mixed plant heights offer habitat for ground beetles, spiders, and other natural pest enemies. This complexity also makes it harder for pests to locate and colonize host plants, reducing the frequency and severity of outbreaks.

Soil functional diversity also contributes to pest suppression. A rich soil biota, including bacteria, fungi, nematodes, and arthropods, competes with or antagonizes soil-borne pests and pathogens. Practices that build soil organic matter and reduce chemical inputs support this living community and its natural regulatory functions.

Crop rotation and polycultures further disrupt pest and disease cycles by breaking the continuity of susceptible host plants. Integrating livestock, where appropriate, can add another layer of diversity, as grazing can interrupt pest habitats and cycle nutrients.

Managing for functional diversity involves thoughtful planning—choosing appropriate crop species, providing continuous habitat, and minimizing broad-spectrum pesticide use. Regular monitoring of pest and beneficial populations guides adaptive management and ensures that ecological processes are maintained.

By leveraging functional diversity, farmers reduce reliance on chemical controls, lower production costs, and foster resilient systems that can adapt to changing pest pressures. Pest regulation rooted in ecosystem function not only protects yields but also enhances the long-term sustainability and health of agricultural landscapes.

Balancing Production and Conservation Goals

Balancing production and conservation goals is at the heart of ecosystem-based agriculture, where the aim is to achieve robust food production while safeguarding the natural systems that make farming possible. Historically, agriculture has often been seen as competing with conservation, with efforts to maximize yields leading to habitat loss, biodiversity decline, and environmental degradation. However, by integrating conservation into agricultural management, it is possible to support both productive farming and healthy ecosystems.

A key strategy is multifunctional land use, where farming systems are designed to deliver a range of outputs beyond food, fiber, or fuel. By incorporating features such as hedgerows, wetlands, buffer strips, and woodlots, farms can maintain habitats for wildlife, regulate water and nutrient flows, and store carbon—while still producing crops and livestock. This approach recognizes the landscape as a mosaic, where different areas serve different but complementary purposes.

Spatial planning is essential to balance these goals. Mapping fields, natural features, and sensitive areas allows for the identification of priority zones for conservation and areas best suited for intensive production. Practices such as conservation tillage, agroforestry, and cover cropping help maintain soil and water resources, even on working lands.

Economic tools also play a role. Diversifying income sources—such as agro-tourism, direct marketing, or payments for ecosystem services—can make conservation efforts financially viable for farmers. Policies and incentives that reward stewardship, support habitat creation, or fund conservation practices help bridge the gap between short-term economic pressures and long-term sustainability.

Collaboration is often needed, especially when conservation objectives span multiple properties or require coordinated action at the landscape scale. Farmers, landowners, conservation groups, and government agencies can work together to design solutions that reflect local priorities and shared benefits.

Monitoring and adaptive management are critical to ensure that both production and conservation goals are being met. Tracking outcomes, learning from experience, and adjusting practices as needed support ongoing improvement.

By embracing integrated management and recognizing the value of both agricultural output and ecological health, it is possible to create landscapes where production and conservation reinforce one another, ensuring resilient food systems and vibrant ecosystems for the future.

Chapter 5: Climate Change Adaptation and Mitigation

Chapter 5 addresses the twin challenges of climate change adaptation and mitigation within agricultural systems. As climate variability intensifies, farmers face increasing risks from droughts, floods, extreme temperatures, and shifting pest and disease pressures. This chapter examines how EBS can help agriculture adapt to these threats by building resilience into production systems and landscapes. It also explores strategies for reducing greenhouse gas emissions and enhancing carbon sequestration through practices like agroforestry, regenerative soil management, and diversified production systems. The discussion highlights the value of climate-smart agriculture principles, ecosystem-based adaptation, and integrated landscape approaches for safeguarding food security and ecosystem health. Chapter 5 equips readers with practical and scalable strategies for making agriculture both a source of climate resilience and a key player in global mitigation efforts.

Climate Risks to Agricultural Systems

Climate risks to agricultural systems are intensifying as global temperatures rise and weather patterns become increasingly unpredictable. Agriculture is particularly vulnerable to changes in climate due to its reliance on stable weather, predictable growing seasons, and the availability of natural resources such as water and fertile soil. Understanding these risks is essential for designing resilient and adaptive farming practices that can withstand a changing climate.

Extreme weather events—such as droughts, floods, heatwaves, and storms—pose immediate threats to crops, livestock, and farm infrastructure. Prolonged drought can reduce soil moisture, stress plants, and diminish yields, while excessive rainfall and flooding can cause waterlogging, soil erosion, and crop loss. Heatwaves can damage sensitive crops, lower pollination rates, and increase water demand, while cold snaps and unseasonal frosts may disrupt flowering and fruiting.

In addition to acute weather events, climate change affects agriculture through gradual shifts in temperature, precipitation patterns, and the frequency of extreme events. Warmer temperatures can alter crop growth cycles, shift planting and harvest dates, and expand the range of pests and diseases. Changing rainfall patterns can lead to water scarcity in some regions and excess in others, making it more challenging to plan for irrigation and drainage.

Climate change also impacts pollinator populations, soil health, and the distribution of invasive species, all of which influence farm productivity. Coastal agricultural areas face added risks from sea-level rise, saltwater intrusion, and increased storm surges, threatening fertile lowland fields and freshwater supplies.

Socioeconomic factors further compound climate risks, as smallholders and resource-poor farmers may lack the resources to adapt to new conditions or recover from losses. These vulnerabilities highlight the need for adaptive strategies and robust support systems.

Recognizing and planning for climate risks enables farmers and land managers to adopt EBS that build resilience—such as diversified cropping, soil and water conservation, and climate-smart management. Proactive adaptation not only safeguards productivity but also helps secure the long-term sustainability of agricultural systems in a rapidly changing world.

Carbon Sequestration in Agricultural Landscapes

Carbon sequestration in agricultural landscapes refers to the process of capturing and storing atmospheric carbon dioxide in soil, vegetation, and other components of the farming ecosystem. This process not only helps mitigate climate change by reducing greenhouse gas concentrations but also delivers significant benefits for soil health, fertility, and overall ecosystem function.

Soil is one of the largest terrestrial carbon sinks, capable of storing more carbon than the atmosphere and vegetation combined. Practices that build soil organic matter—such as cover cropping, reduced tillage, organic amendments, and maintaining perennial vegetation—enhance the soil's capacity to capture and retain carbon. As plant residues decompose, carbon becomes incorporated into soil organic matter, where it can remain stable for years or even centuries.

Agroforestry and the integration of trees into farmland further increase carbon storage. Trees absorb carbon dioxide through photosynthesis and store it in their trunks, branches, roots, and leaves. Planting shelterbelts, windbreaks, or hedgerows, as well as establishing orchards or silvopasture systems, adds additional carbon sinks across the landscape.

Restoring degraded lands and wetlands within agricultural areas also contributes to carbon sequestration. Healthy wetlands trap organic carbon in their saturated soils, while restoration efforts can reverse historical losses and increase overall landscape carbon stocks. Similarly, converting marginal or unproductive lands to native grasslands or forests removes carbon from the atmosphere and supports biodiversity.

Effective carbon sequestration strategies require careful management to maximize benefits and avoid unintended consequences. For example, avoiding excessive soil disturbance preserves stored carbon, while thoughtful species selection and landscape design ensure resilience and productivity. Monitoring and adaptive management help maintain carbon gains over time.

Beyond climate mitigation, carbon-rich soils and vegetated landscapes are more resilient to drought, erosion, and nutrient loss, supporting long-term agricultural productivity. Participation in carbon markets or incentive programs can also provide additional income streams for farmers adopting climate-friendly practices.

By prioritizing carbon sequestration, agricultural landscapes become active contributors to climate solutions while enhancing ecosystem services, soil fertility, and farm viability for future generations.

Agroforestry and Carbon Farming

Agroforestry and carbon farming are complementary approaches that enhance the capacity of agricultural landscapes to capture and store carbon, while also delivering co-benefits for biodiversity, productivity, and climate resilience. By integrating trees, shrubs, and perennial plants with crops and livestock, agroforestry systems create multifunctional landscapes that mimic natural ecosystems and strengthen the ecological foundation of agriculture.

In agroforestry systems, trees absorb atmospheric carbon dioxide through photosynthesis and store it in their wood, roots, and leaves. This carbon is further transferred to the soil as leaf litter and root biomass decompose, building soil organic matter and increasing overall carbon stocks. Practices such as alley cropping, silvopasture, shelterbelts, and forest farming all contribute to carbon sequestration while supporting diverse farm outputs.

Carbon farming refers to the intentional adoption of agricultural practices that increase the storage of carbon in soils and vegetation. Alongside agroforestry, carbon farming may include conservation tillage, cover cropping, use of organic amendments, and restoration of degraded lands. These strategies not only remove carbon from the atmosphere but also improve soil health, water retention, and nutrient cycling.

The integration of trees and perennial plants in agricultural landscapes supports habitat for wildlife, enhances pollination and pest regulation, and creates microclimates that protect crops from extreme weather. Agroforestry and carbon farming also help prevent soil erosion, reduce water runoff, and buffer fields against drought and flooding.

For farmers, these approaches offer economic and ecological incentives. In addition to diversified products such as timber, fruit, fodder, and medicinal plants, farmers can participate in carbon credit or payment for ecosystem services programs, generating additional income from their climate-positive practices.

Successful agroforestry and carbon farming require careful planning—selecting suitable tree and plant species, considering spacing and compatibility with existing crops or livestock, and managing for long-term balance and resilience. Ongoing monitoring and adaptive management ensure that carbon gains are maintained and that ecological benefits continue to accrue.

By adopting agroforestry and carbon farming, agricultural systems become more sustainable and climate-friendly, contributing to global efforts to mitigate greenhouse gas emissions and build resilient food production systems.

Climate-Smart Agriculture Principles

Climate-smart agriculture (CSA) encompasses a set of guiding principles and practices designed to transform and reorient agricultural systems in response to the challenges posed by climate change. The core aim of CSA is to achieve three interconnected objectives: sustainably increasing agricultural productivity and incomes, adapting and building resilience to climate change, and reducing or removing greenhouse gas emissions wherever possible.

A foundational principle of CSA is the adoption of integrated, systems-based approaches. Rather than focusing on single solutions, CSA encourages the coordination of crop, livestock, soil, and water management to maximize synergies and minimize trade-offs. This holistic perspective helps build resilience in the face of climate variability and uncertainty.

Diversification is another key tenet of climate-smart agriculture. By growing a range of crops, integrating livestock, and incorporating agroforestry, farms spread risk and increase their adaptive capacity. Diversified systems are better able to withstand shocks from extreme weather events, pest outbreaks, or market fluctuations, ensuring more stable yields and livelihoods.

Resource-use efficiency lies at the heart of CSA. Practices such as precision irrigation, conservation tillage, integrated nutrient management, and the use of drought- or heat-tolerant crop varieties help optimize the use of water, energy, and inputs. Efficient management not only conserves resources but also reduces production costs and environmental impacts.

Building soil health is central to climate resilience. Maintaining ground cover, enhancing organic matter, and minimizing disturbance improve water retention, nutrient cycling, and resistance to erosion and degradation. Healthy soils are more resilient to drought and can sequester more carbon, supporting both adaptation and mitigation goals.

Climate-smart agriculture also prioritizes information, innovation, and knowledge sharing. Using weather forecasts, climate models, and early warning systems enables better planning and risk management. Farmer education, participatory research, and extension services foster local adaptation and the uptake of climate-smart practices.

Policy support, institutional coordination, and access to finance are essential for scaling CSA. Incentives, insurance, and investment in infrastructure help lower barriers to adoption and create enabling environments.

By embracing climate-smart principles, agricultural systems can remain productive and resilient, supporting both food security and environmental sustainability in a rapidly changing world.

Ecosystem-Based Adaptation Strategies

Ecosystem-based adaptation (EbA) strategies leverage the functions and services of natural systems to help agriculture cope with the impacts of climate change. These approaches focus on harnessing biodiversity, ecological processes, and landscape management to reduce vulnerability, increase resilience, and sustain productivity in the face of climate-related stresses such as drought, floods, temperature extremes, and shifting growing conditions.

One core strategy is restoring and conserving natural habitats within and around farmland. Forests, wetlands, riparian buffers, and grasslands provide ecological buffers that absorb excess water during heavy rainfall, reduce the risk of flooding, and stabilize soils against erosion. These habitats also moderate microclimates, protect crops from wind and temperature extremes, and support the pollinators and natural enemies of pests needed for robust food production.

Diversifying production systems—through crop rotation, intercropping, agroforestry, and integrating livestock—strengthens adaptive capacity. Diverse systems spread risk and enable farms to respond more flexibly to climatic variability, pests, and diseases. Planting drought-tolerant or heat-resistant crop varieties, managing planting dates, and adjusting rotations help ensure continued yields under changing conditions.

Soil and water conservation practices are also central to EbA. Techniques such as cover cropping, conservation tillage, mulching, and water harvesting enhance soil moisture retention, improve infiltration, and maintain soil structure. These actions help buffer crops against drought, reduce runoff, and maintain water availability during dry spells.

Landscape-level adaptation integrates individual farm efforts with broader management of watersheds, corridors, and ecosystems. Coordinating activities across multiple properties ensures the connectivity and function of ecological networks that underpin resilience.

Engaging local communities, drawing on traditional knowledge, and involving stakeholders in planning and implementation are essential for the success of EbA strategies. Participatory approaches ensure that solutions are context-specific, culturally appropriate, and supported by those who depend on the land.

By adopting ecosystem-based adaptation strategies, agricultural systems can reduce their exposure to climate risks while maintaining the natural capital needed for long-term productivity. EbA provides a pathway for building resilient, sustainable agriculture in a world of accelerating environmental change.

Reducing Greenhouse Gas Emissions

Reducing greenhouse gas (GHG) emissions in agriculture is a critical component of climate mitigation and a core element of EBS. Agricultural activities produce significant amounts of carbon dioxide, methane, and nitrous oxide—gases that contribute to global warming. Effective emission reduction strategies combine improved management practices, technological innovation, and ecological approaches to minimize the carbon footprint of food production while maintaining productivity.

One major source of GHGs in agriculture is soil management, particularly the use of synthetic fertilizers and intensive tillage. By adopting precision nutrient management, farmers can apply fertilizers at the right rate, time, and method to meet crop needs while minimizing excess application that leads to nitrous oxide emissions. Incorporating legumes, cover crops, and organic amendments into rotations further reduces dependence on synthetic inputs and supports natural nutrient cycling.

Methane emissions, primarily from livestock and flooded rice paddies, can be addressed through improved feeding strategies, manure management, and water-saving irrigation techniques. For example, altering cattle diets to include more digestible forages or feed additives can reduce enteric fermentation, while composting or anaerobic digestion of manure captures methane for use as renewable energy. Intermittent drying of rice fields—known as alternate wetting and drying—lowers methane production compared to continuous flooding.

Reducing tillage and maintaining permanent soil cover help sequester carbon in soils and reduce emissions from soil disturbance. Agroforestry and tree planting within agricultural systems also remove carbon dioxide from the atmosphere, storing it in woody biomass and enhancing farm resilience.

Energy efficiency and the adoption of renewable energy on farms, such as solar-powered irrigation or machinery, further decrease GHG emissions associated with fossil fuel use.

Supporting these technical measures with strong extension services, financial incentives, and access to information enables farmers to make informed decisions and invest in climate-friendly practices. Monitoring and reporting tools help track progress and guide adaptive management.

Through a combination of ecological, technological, and management innovations, agriculture can significantly reduce its greenhouse gas emissions. These actions contribute to global climate goals while building more efficient, resilient, and sustainable food production systems.

Building Climate-Resilient Food Systems

Building climate-resilient food systems is essential for ensuring stable and sustainable food production in the face of increasing climate variability and extreme weather events. A climate-resilient food system is one that can anticipate, absorb, and recover from climate shocks while maintaining its essential functions of providing safe, nutritious, and accessible food for all. Achieving this resilience requires a combination of ecosystem-based approaches, technological innovations, and strong social networks.

At the farm level, diversification of crops, livestock, and income sources spreads risk and enhances adaptive capacity. Integrating climate-smart practices—such as conservation tillage, agroforestry, water harvesting, and soil health management—improves resource use efficiency and buffers against the effects of drought, floods, and temperature extremes. Growing a wider range of species and varieties reduces the likelihood of total crop failure when weather or pests threaten a particular crop.

Robust seed systems and the use of stress-tolerant, locally adapted crop varieties enable farmers to adjust planting schedules and choose crops that are better suited to changing conditions. Developing and conserving seed diversity supports both immediate adaptation and long-term resilience as climates continue to evolve.

Access to timely information—such as weather forecasts, early warning systems, and market trends—empowers farmers and communities to make informed decisions and respond proactively to emerging threats. Digital platforms, extension services, and participatory networks facilitate the sharing of knowledge and innovations, accelerating the adoption of climate-resilient practices.

Infrastructure, such as reliable irrigation, storage, and transportation systems, increases the stability and efficiency of food supply chains. Social safety nets, crop insurance, and risk-sharing mechanisms provide financial support that helps farmers and vulnerable populations recover from losses and rebuild livelihoods after climate-related shocks.

Building resilience also depends on enabling policies and institutions. Integrating climate adaptation and disaster risk management into agricultural planning, providing incentives for EBS, and fostering collaboration among stakeholders strengthen the entire food system.

By combining ecological, technological, and social strategies, climate-resilient food systems become better able to withstand and recover from climate impacts. This approach not only secures food supplies but also protects natural resources and rural communities, ensuring a stable and sustainable food future in a changing climate.

Chapter 6: Integrated Pest and Disease Management

Chapter 6 examines the role of integrated pest and disease management as a cornerstone of sustainable, ecosystem-based agriculture. Pests and diseases pose persistent threats to crop yields and farm profitability, but traditional reliance on chemical controls can undermine ecosystem health and foster resistance. This chapter explores ecological principles and practical strategies for managing pests and diseases by harnessing biodiversity, functional diversity, and natural regulatory processes. It covers biological control methods, crop and landscape diversification, pest-resistant crop varieties, and the enhancement of natural enemies. The discussion highlights the importance of monitoring, adaptive management, and reducing chemical inputs to create resilient, self-regulating agroecosystems. By integrating these approaches, farmers can achieve effective pest and disease control while maintaining productivity and protecting the environment.

Ecological Basis for Pest and Disease Control

The ecological basis for pest and disease control in agriculture centers on leveraging natural processes and relationships within ecosystems to suppress pests and pathogens, rather than relying solely on chemical interventions. Healthy, diverse ecosystems contain a variety of organisms that interact in complex ways, providing natural checks and balances that keep pest populations and disease outbreaks under control.

Biodiversity is a fundamental component of ecological pest and disease management. Diverse plantings attract beneficial insects such as predators, parasitoids, and pollinators that prey on or disrupt pest species. These natural enemies, including lady beetles, spiders, and parasitic wasps, help keep pest numbers below damaging thresholds, reducing the need for insecticides. Similarly, maintaining a variety of plant species in and around fields can interrupt the life cycles of crop pests and diseases by making it harder for them to locate suitable hosts or by harboring antagonistic microbes.

Soil health also plays a critical role in disease suppression. Soils rich in organic matter and teeming with microorganisms support beneficial fungi and bacteria that compete with or inhibit plant pathogens. Practices that increase soil biodiversity, such as cover cropping, compost application, and minimal tillage, enhance this natural disease resistance and reduce dependence on chemical fungicides.

Habitat manipulation, including the establishment of hedgerows, buffer strips, and conservation headlands, provides additional refuges and resources for beneficial species. Creating these habitats in agricultural landscapes increases the abundance and diversity of natural enemies and supports the persistence of ecological pest control.

IPM builds on these ecological principles by combining biological, cultural, physical, and—when necessary—chemical controls in a holistic approach. Regular monitoring and adaptive management ensure that interventions are timely, targeted, and compatible with ecosystem health.

By understanding and applying the ecological basis for pest and disease control, farmers can foster resilient systems that suppress pests and pathogens naturally, minimize input costs, and protect the environment. This approach not only sustains productivity but also enhances the long-term sustainability and health of agricultural landscapes.

Biological Control Methods

Biological control methods are essential components of ecosystem-based pest and disease management in agriculture, relying on the use of living organisms to suppress pest populations and reduce crop losses. This approach harnesses the natural relationships between pests and their predators, parasites, or pathogens to maintain ecological balance and minimize the need for synthetic chemical pesticides.

There are three main types of biological control: classical, augmentative, and conservation. Classical biological control involves introducing a natural enemy of a pest species from its native range into a new environment where the pest has become problematic. This method is often used for invasive pests lacking effective local predators, aiming to establish a self-sustaining population of the control agent.

Augmentative biological control enhances the existing population of beneficial organisms by releasing additional individuals at critical times. This can involve mass-rearing and releasing predators or parasitoids to target a specific pest outbreak. These releases may be inoculative—establishing the control agent early in the season—or inundative, where large numbers are released to provide immediate pest suppression.

Conservation biological control focuses on preserving and enhancing the populations of native or already established beneficial organisms. Farmers achieve this by minimizing pesticide use, providing habitats such as flower strips, hedgerows, or beetle banks, and maintaining diverse cropping systems that supply food and shelter for natural enemies.

Biological control is most effective when combined with other pest management strategies, such as crop rotation, resistant varieties, and habitat manipulation, in an IPM framework. Regular monitoring of pest and beneficial populations is crucial to assess effectiveness and make timely decisions.

Using biological control methods reduces reliance on broad-spectrum chemical pesticides, lowering the risks of environmental contamination, pesticide resistance, and non-target effects on beneficial species. It also supports pollinator health and conserves biodiversity in agricultural landscapes.

By adopting biological control as a cornerstone of pest management, farmers can achieve sustainable crop protection that is environmentally sound, economically viable, and resilient to the challenges posed by evolving pest pressures and changing climate conditions.

Crop and Landscape Diversification for Pest Suppression

Crop and landscape diversification are key strategies for suppressing pests and enhancing the ecological balance of agricultural systems. By increasing the variety of crops and habitat features both within and around fields, farmers disrupt pest life cycles, encourage natural enemies, and build more resilient agroecosystems.

Crop diversification involves growing different species or varieties in rotation, intercropping, or polycultures rather than relying on single-crop monocultures. Rotating crops changes the availability of host plants for pests and diseases, interrupting their reproduction and reducing the buildup of pest populations in the soil or on plant debris. Intercropping—planting two or more crops together—confuses pests, making it harder for them to locate their preferred hosts and decreasing the likelihood of severe outbreaks.

Landscape diversification expands the approach to the farm or regional scale. Incorporating features such as hedgerows, wildflower strips, woodlots, and wetlands increases habitat complexity and provides resources for beneficial insects, birds, and other pest predators. These natural enemies use diversified landscapes for food, shelter, and reproduction, resulting in enhanced biological control and lower pest pressure.

Maintaining uncultivated field margins and conserving patches of native vegetation also support pollinators and beneficial insects while acting as barriers to pest movement. Diverse vegetation structures and microhabitats promote the persistence and movement of natural enemies across the landscape, ensuring their availability when pest populations rise.

Integrating livestock, agroforestry, or perennial crops adds further complexity, disrupting pest habitats and life cycles while recycling nutrients and strengthening system resilience. The presence of multiple plant types and varied habitats can also reduce the risk of pest adaptation and resistance, extending the effectiveness of biological control measures.

Effective diversification requires planning and knowledge of local pest species, beneficial organisms, and crop compatibility. Regular monitoring and adaptive management help optimize diversification strategies for pest suppression.

By promoting crop and landscape diversity, farmers create dynamic agricultural systems that are less vulnerable to pest outbreaks and more sustainable in the long term. These approaches support both productivity and ecological health, forming a cornerstone of ecosystem-based pest management.

Enhancing Natural Enemies of Pests

Enhancing natural enemies of pests is a cornerstone of ecosystem-based pest management, focusing on strengthening the populations and effectiveness of organisms that prey on, parasitize, or otherwise suppress crop pests. These natural enemies—such as predatory insects, spiders, parasitoid wasps, birds, bats, and beneficial microbes—play a critical role in maintaining ecological balance and reducing the need for chemical interventions in agricultural systems.

Habitat management is a primary strategy for supporting natural enemies. Providing a diversity of flowering plants, hedgerows, cover crops, and uncultivated field margins ensures a continuous supply of nectar, pollen, alternative prey, and shelter. These resources are especially important during periods when target pests are scarce, helping beneficial populations persist throughout the growing season.

Reducing pesticide use, especially broad-spectrum chemicals, protects non-target organisms and enables natural enemy populations to flourish. When chemical control is necessary, selecting targeted products and using them judiciously can minimize harm to beneficial species. Integrating pest management practices—such as crop rotation, intercropping, and conservation tillage—further disrupts pest life cycles and supports diverse communities of natural enemies.

Releasing commercially reared beneficial insects, such as lady beetles or parasitoid wasps, can augment existing populations and provide rapid pest suppression during outbreaks. These introductions are most effective when combined with habitat enhancements and conservation practices that support their establishment and persistence.

Landscape-level approaches, including the creation of ecological corridors and the maintenance of native vegetation patches, facilitate the movement and dispersal of natural enemies across farms and fields. This connectivity helps ensure that beneficial organisms can respond quickly to pest outbreaks and exert effective control over larger areas.

Monitoring pest and natural enemy populations allows for adaptive management, ensuring that interventions are well-timed and support ecological processes. Training and collaboration among farmers, extension agents, and researchers further enhance the success of these strategies.

By fostering robust populations of natural enemies, farmers reduce reliance on synthetic pesticides, lower production costs, and promote resilient, self-regulating agricultural ecosystems. Enhancing natural enemies is a vital component of sustainable pest management and long-term farm health.

Reducing Reliance on Chemical Inputs

Reducing reliance on chemical inputs is a fundamental goal of ecosystem-based agriculture, offering multiple benefits for environmental health, farm sustainability, and food safety. The overuse of synthetic fertilizers, herbicides, and pesticides has contributed to soil degradation, water pollution, loss of biodiversity, and the development of resistant pest and weed populations. Shifting toward integrated, ecological approaches allows farmers to maintain productivity while minimizing negative externalities.

A first step is the adoption of IPM, which emphasizes prevention, monitoring, and targeted control measures. IPM combines cultural, biological, mechanical, and, when necessary, minimal chemical controls to manage pests within economic thresholds rather than seeking complete eradication. Regular field scouting and pest population assessments guide timely, informed interventions.

Nutrient management is equally important. Soil testing and site-specific recommendations enable precise application of fertilizers, reducing waste and runoff. Incorporating organic amendments such as compost, manure, and green manures not only supplies nutrients but also enhances soil structure and microbial activity, making nutrients more available to plants and less prone to loss.

Weed control strategies can be diversified through crop rotation, cover cropping, mulching, and mechanical cultivation. These practices disrupt weed life cycles, suppress germination, and reduce competition without sole reliance on herbicides.

Biological control harnesses natural predators, parasitoids, and pathogens to keep pest populations in check. Providing habitat for beneficial organisms and maintaining diverse plantings strengthen these natural regulatory services.

Reducing tillage and maintaining ground cover with residues or living plants improve soil health and suppress pests and weeds, decreasing the need for chemical interventions. Selecting disease-resistant crop varieties and implementing sound sanitation measures further reduce vulnerability to outbreaks.

Education, farmer networks, and extension support are vital for sharing knowledge and innovations that facilitate the transition away from chemical dependency. Policy incentives, certification schemes, and market rewards for sustainably produced products can accelerate adoption.

By minimizing chemical input use and embracing ecosystem-based alternatives, farmers protect natural resources, reduce production costs, and deliver safer, more nutritious food. This shift strengthens the resilience and sustainability of agriculture while safeguarding the health of people and the environment.

Pest-Resistant Crop Varieties

Pest-resistant crop varieties are a vital tool in the ecological management of agricultural pests, supporting productivity and reducing the need for chemical interventions. Through traditional breeding, modern biotechnology, or the selection of naturally resilient plants, these varieties possess traits that make them less susceptible to damage from specific insects, pathogens, or nematodes. Their use enhances the resilience of cropping systems and supports the broader goals of ecosystem-based agriculture.

Selecting pest-resistant varieties starts with understanding local pest pressures and environmental conditions. Plant breeders identify and incorporate traits such as physical barriers, like thicker cuticles or hairs, and biochemical defenses, including naturally occurring toxins or repellents, to deter or withstand pest attacks. Resistance can be either complete, where the plant prevents pest establishment, or partial, reducing pest survival and reproduction without eliminating them entirely.

Deploying resistant varieties as part of an IPM strategy provides reliable, season-long protection and lowers the risk of sudden outbreaks. These varieties help stabilize yields, especially where pest problems are chronic or unpredictable, and they enable farmers to decrease reliance on pesticides, lowering production costs and environmental impacts.

Genetic diversity among crops further enhances system resilience. Rotating different resistant varieties or stacking multiple resistance genes within the same variety can slow the adaptation of pests and pathogens. Using locally adapted, open-pollinated, or heirloom varieties maintains a pool of genetic traits that may offer resistance to emerging threats under changing climate conditions.

The development and deployment of pest-resistant varieties benefit from close collaboration among plant breeders, researchers, extension agents, and farmers. Participatory breeding programs ensure that varieties meet local needs and preferences, facilitating adoption and maximizing effectiveness.

Regulatory approval and stewardship are important considerations, especially for genetically modified or transgenic crops. Stewardship practices, such as planting refuge areas of non-resistant crops, help delay resistance development in pest populations.

Integrating pest-resistant crop varieties with ecological and cultural controls, habitat management, and regular monitoring forms a robust and sustainable approach to pest management. This strategy strengthens agricultural systems, stabilizes yields, and promotes the long-term health of farms and ecosystems.

Monitoring and Adaptive Management

Monitoring and adaptive management are crucial components of effective ecosystem-based pest and disease control, ensuring that agricultural systems remain resilient and productive over time. Rather than relying on static prescriptions or routine chemical applications, these approaches emphasize observation, learning, and flexible response to changing conditions and emerging threats.

Monitoring involves the systematic collection of data on pest and disease incidence, crop health, environmental conditions, and the presence of natural enemies. Field scouting, traps, and diagnostic tests provide real-time information about pest populations and disease outbreaks. Technology, such as remote sensing, drones, and digital data platforms, enhances the accuracy and efficiency of monitoring efforts, enabling timely and site-specific decisions.

Threshold-based action is a key principle. Instead of responding to every pest presence, interventions are triggered only when populations reach levels likely to cause economic damage. This targeted approach minimizes unnecessary inputs and supports ecological balance, allowing beneficial organisms to persist and contribute to pest regulation.

Adaptive management builds on this foundation by treating farm management as an ongoing process of experimentation, assessment, and adjustment. Farmers and land managers set clear objectives, implement strategies, and continuously evaluate outcomes. When monitoring reveals that current practices are not meeting targets or that new threats have emerged, management strategies are adjusted accordingly.

Feedback loops are central to adaptive management. Lessons learned from past actions inform future decisions, promoting innovation and continuous improvement. Collaboration with extension services, researchers, and farmer networks strengthens knowledge exchange and supports the development of locally relevant solutions.

Documentation and data analysis play important roles in tracking progress and guiding change. Detailed records help identify patterns, evaluate the effectiveness of interventions, and refine decision-making processes.

Institutional support, technical assistance, and access to user-friendly monitoring tools are important for scaling up these practices. Policies and incentive programs can further encourage farmers to adopt adaptive, ecosystem-based approaches.

Employing monitoring and adaptive management enables farms to respond dynamically to pests and diseases, maintain ecological balance, and reduce reliance on chemical controls. These practices foster more resilient, sustainable agricultural systems that can thrive under variable and changing environmental conditions.

Chapter 7: Sustainable Intensification and Productivity

Chapter 7 explores the concept of sustainable intensification as a pathway to increasing agricultural productivity while preserving environmental integrity. As demand for food rises, there is growing pressure to produce more from existing farmland without expanding into natural ecosystems. This chapter examines ecosystem-based intensification pathways that harness ecological processes, improve resource use efficiency, and support diversified production systems. It discusses the importance of nutrient cycling, closed-loop systems, and linking productivity with positive environmental outcomes. By emphasizing integrated, multifunctional approaches, Chapter 7 demonstrates how farms can boost yields, enhance resilience, and regenerate natural resources. The discussion offers practical guidance for balancing production goals with sustainability, highlighting strategies that enable agriculture to meet global needs without compromising the health of future generations or the planet.

Defining Sustainable Intensification in Agriculture

Sustainable intensification in agriculture refers to increasing food production from existing farmland while minimizing negative environmental impacts and preserving natural resources for future generations. This approach seeks to reconcile the need for higher yields with the imperative of sustainability, emphasizing efficient resource use, ecosystem health, and social equity alongside productivity gains.

The core of sustainable intensification lies in producing more with less. It involves adopting practices and technologies that boost yields, reduce waste, and optimize the use of inputs such as water, nutrients, and energy. Rather than expanding farmland into forests, grasslands, or wetlands, sustainable intensification focuses on enhancing productivity on current agricultural land through science-based innovations and ecological principles.

Key components include precision agriculture, which uses data and technology to match inputs precisely to crop needs, and conservation agriculture, which reduces soil disturbance, maintains permanent cover, and rotates crops to maintain soil health. Improved crop varieties, IPM, efficient irrigation, and soil fertility management all contribute to increased output without degrading the land or environment.

Sustainable intensification also prioritizes the preservation of ecosystem services—such as pollination, water regulation, and nutrient cycling—that underpin agricultural productivity. Multifunctional landscapes that integrate trees, wetlands, and biodiversity conservation provide additional benefits beyond food production, including climate mitigation and resilience to extreme weather events.

Social and economic dimensions are equally important. Sustainable intensification aims to support livelihoods, promote gender equity, and ensure that smallholder farmers and rural communities benefit from increased productivity. Access to knowledge, credit, markets, and decision-making processes is vital for equitable outcomes.

Monitoring, adaptive management, and a commitment to continuous learning help ensure that intensification remains truly sustainable, avoiding unintended consequences such as increased pollution or loss of biodiversity.

Sustainable intensification does not prescribe a single pathway but encourages context-specific solutions based on local conditions, needs, and priorities. This flexible, integrated approach creates a foundation for feeding a growing population while safeguarding the natural systems that agriculture—and society—depend on.

Ecosystem-Based Intensification Pathways

Ecosystem-based intensification pathways center on harnessing ecological processes to increase agricultural productivity in a sustainable manner. These pathways move beyond traditional input-intensive approaches, focusing instead on optimizing the interactions among crops, soils, water, biodiversity, and climate within farming systems. The goal is to produce more food while enhancing ecosystem services and maintaining environmental integrity.

A key pathway involves building healthy soils as the foundation of productive and resilient agriculture. Practices such as reduced tillage, cover cropping, organic amendments, and diversified crop rotations foster robust soil microbial communities, improve structure, and increase nutrient cycling. Healthier soils retain more water and nutrients, support plant growth, and reduce the need for synthetic fertilizers.

Increasing on-farm biodiversity is another crucial aspect. Integrating a variety of crops, livestock, and trees within the same landscape promotes functional diversity and supports natural pest control, pollination, and nutrient cycling. Agroforestry, intercropping, and silvopasture systems exemplify how biodiversity can be used to intensify production without compromising sustainability.

Efficient resource management is central to ecosystem-based intensification. Precision irrigation, water harvesting, and soil moisture monitoring help optimize water use, while targeted nutrient application and organic sources improve fertilizer efficiency. These practices reduce waste, lower costs, and limit negative environmental impacts.

Landscape-level approaches enhance connectivity and ecological function. Maintaining habitat corridors, buffer strips, and wetlands within and around farms supports beneficial wildlife, mitigates runoff, and increases resilience to climate extremes. Managing entire watersheds or catchments ensures that intensification efforts are coordinated and support broader ecological health.

Innovation and knowledge-sharing drive ecosystem-based intensification. Drawing on both scientific research and traditional

71

knowledge enables the development of locally appropriate solutions. Participatory approaches and farmer-to-farmer learning accelerate adoption and adaptation of best practices.

Socioeconomic considerations are integrated into these pathways, ensuring that intensification benefits rural livelihoods, food security, and community well-being. Supportive policies, access to finance, and extension services facilitate widespread adoption.

Ecosystem-based intensification pathways offer a framework for producing more with less, securing agricultural productivity while regenerating the resources and services that future farming depends on.

Resource Use Efficiency and Closed-Loop Systems

Resource use efficiency and closed-loop systems are central to sustainable intensification, enabling farms to optimize inputs, reduce waste, and maintain productive systems with minimal environmental impact. Improving the efficiency of water, nutrients, energy, and other resources not only enhances yields but also lowers production costs and reduces the footprint of agriculture on natural ecosystems.

Water use efficiency is achieved through practices such as precision irrigation, soil moisture monitoring, mulching, and the selection of drought-tolerant crops. These strategies ensure that water is applied where and when it is needed most, minimizing losses to evaporation and runoff. Efficient irrigation systems, such as drip or micro-irrigation, deliver water directly to plant roots, maximizing uptake and reducing waste.

Nutrient management is another pillar of resource use efficiency. Applying fertilizers and organic amendments based on soil testing and crop needs reduces over-application and nutrient leaching. Cover cropping, crop rotation, and the integration of legumes improve soil fertility naturally, while composting and recycling crop residues return valuable nutrients to the soil.

Energy efficiency can be enhanced through reduced tillage, the use of renewable energy sources (such as solar or wind), and careful management of machinery and transport. Efficient farm design, timely operations, and the adoption of energy-saving technologies further cut fuel use and greenhouse gas emissions.

Closed-loop systems take efficiency a step further by designing agricultural operations to recycle and reuse resources wherever possible. Nutrient cycling is maximized through composting, manure management, and the integration of crops and livestock. On-farm water harvesting, wastewater reuse, and the use of organic by-products for animal feed or energy production all contribute to circularity.

Waste reduction and the transformation of by-products into valuable inputs create more self-sufficient farms that depend less on external resources and generate fewer pollutants. Closed-loop systems also build soil organic matter, improve resilience, and support broader ecosystem health.

Implementing resource use efficiency and closed-loop systems requires planning, monitoring, and innovation, but the benefits extend across productivity, profitability, and sustainability. These strategies form a core part of ecosystem-based intensification, advancing agriculture that is both productive and environmentally sound.

Nutrient Cycling and Integrated Fertility Management

Nutrient cycling and integrated fertility management are fundamental to maintaining productive, resilient, and sustainable agricultural systems. Efficient nutrient cycling ensures that essential elements—such as nitrogen, phosphorus, and potassium—are made available to crops in the right amounts and at the right times, while minimizing losses to the environment. Integrated fertility management combines organic and inorganic nutrient sources with management practices that optimize soil health, crop nutrition, and ecosystem function.

In healthy agricultural systems, nutrients cycle through plants, animals, soil organisms, and organic matter. Crop residues, cover crops, animal manures, compost, and green manures return valuable nutrients to the soil as they decompose. Soil microorganisms and fauna, including bacteria, fungi, and earthworms, play crucial roles in breaking down organic matter and converting nutrients into forms that plants can absorb.

Legumes—such as clover, vetch, and beans—fix atmospheric nitrogen through their association with rhizobia bacteria, enriching the soil naturally and reducing the need for synthetic fertilizers. Crop rotations and intercropping with legumes further support nutrient cycling, balance soil fertility, and break pest and disease cycles.

Integrated fertility management relies on regular soil testing to assess nutrient status and inform precise fertilizer application. Applying nutrients based on crop needs prevents overuse, reduces leaching and runoff, and lowers production costs. The use of slow-release or stabilized fertilizers, along with the timing of applications to match crop uptake, further improves efficiency and environmental outcomes.

Incorporating organic amendments—such as compost, manure, and biochar—enhances soil organic matter, supports soil structure, and boosts water and nutrient retention. These materials also stimulate beneficial microbial activity, building long-term fertility and resilience.

Managing soil pH and avoiding excessive tillage maintain conditions favorable for nutrient cycling and root growth. Mulching and maintaining ground cover help protect the soil and prevent nutrient loss.

Integrated approaches that link nutrient cycling with soil health and crop management sustain yields, reduce dependency on external inputs, and minimize negative environmental impacts. This strategy forms the foundation of ecosystem-based agriculture, supporting productive, regenerative, and climate-resilient farming systems.

Diversified Production Systems

Diversified production systems are at the core of sustainable intensification and ecosystem-based agriculture, offering a range of ecological, economic, and social benefits. By integrating multiple crops, livestock, trees, or aquaculture within the same farming operation, diversified systems enhance resilience, improve resource use efficiency, and support broader ecosystem services.

Growing a variety of crops—through intercropping, polycultures, or sequential planting—creates more complex habitats that support beneficial insects, pollinators, and soil organisms. This biological diversity disrupts pest and disease cycles, reduces outbreaks, and improves pollination, leading to more stable and higher yields over time. Diversified cropping also spreads risk, ensuring that failure or market downturns affecting one crop do not devastate the entire farm.

Incorporating livestock adds further value by cycling nutrients, improving pasture health, and providing additional income streams. Manure from animals enriches soil organic matter and fertility, while rotational grazing enhances plant diversity and soil structure. Fish farming or integrated aquaculture systems can be combined with crops and livestock, recycling water and nutrients and providing protein-rich food.

Agroforestry—blending trees with crops and/or livestock—offers shade, wind protection, and additional products such as fruit, nuts, timber, or fuelwood. Trees sequester carbon, stabilize soil, and improve microclimates, contributing to climate resilience and farm sustainability.

Diversified systems can be adapted to local environments, market opportunities, and cultural practices. Home gardens, mixed farming, and community-supported agriculture are all examples that support household nutrition, local economies, and social cohesion.

Successful implementation requires careful planning, knowledge of species compatibility, and adaptive management to optimize interactions and minimize competition for resources. Access to diverse markets, technical support, and appropriate infrastructure are important for realizing the full benefits of diversification.

Ecological intensification through diversified production systems enhances productivity, conserves natural resources, and buffers against economic and environmental shocks. These systems represent a path toward regenerative, resilient agriculture that delivers food security, livelihoods, and ecosystem health for both current and future generations.

Linking Productivity and Environmental Outcomes

Linking productivity and environmental outcomes is a central challenge and opportunity in ecosystem-based agriculture. Traditional agricultural models often treat yield maximization and environmental stewardship as competing goals. However, well-designed systems demonstrate that high productivity and positive environmental impacts can be mutually reinforcing, creating a virtuous cycle that supports both farm profitability and ecosystem health.

Integrated management practices play a key role in achieving this balance. Techniques such as crop rotation, cover cropping, reduced tillage, and precision nutrient management not only enhance yields but also build soil fertility, improve water retention, and reduce nutrient losses. These practices contribute to more robust harvests while minimizing runoff, erosion, and the depletion of natural resources.

Agroforestry, buffer strips, and the maintenance of non-cropped habitats within the farm landscape offer additional benefits. These features support pollinators, pest predators, and soil organisms that are essential for crop productivity. At the same time, they help filter runoff, store carbon, and conserve biodiversity, reinforcing the farm's environmental foundation.

Water management is another area where productivity and environmental gains align. Efficient irrigation systems, water harvesting, and practices that maintain soil organic matter enable crops to thrive with less water and reduce stress on local water supplies. Healthy soils act as reservoirs, supporting both crop growth and downstream ecosystem health.

Monitoring and feedback systems are essential for optimizing the relationship between productivity and environmental outcomes. Regular assessment of soil health, water quality, pest dynamics, and yields allows for adaptive management and continuous improvement. Information sharing and collaboration among farmers, researchers, and advisors help scale up effective practices.

Economic incentives, such as payments for ecosystem services, certification schemes, and market premiums for sustainably produced products, further encourage practices that deliver both productive and environmental benefits.

Ecosystem-based agriculture demonstrates that it is possible to achieve high yields while regenerating natural resources and reducing negative impacts. Systems that link productivity with environmental outcomes are more resilient, sustainable, and capable of meeting society's growing demand for food and ecosystem services in a changing world.

Scaling Up Sustainable Intensification Practices

Scaling up sustainable intensification practices is essential for transforming agricultural systems to meet global food demand while safeguarding the environment and enhancing rural livelihoods. Moving from isolated success stories to widespread adoption requires coordinated efforts across multiple levels—farm, community, policy, and market—and the integration of technical, institutional, and social innovations.

At the farm level, scaling up involves expanding the use of proven practices such as conservation agriculture, agroforestry, IPM, resource-efficient irrigation, and diversified production systems. Farmers benefit from access to knowledge, training, and demonstration sites that showcase the effectiveness and adaptability of these approaches in real-world conditions.

Community-level actions foster collective learning and resource sharing. Farmer field schools, cooperatives, and peer-to-peer networks accelerate the dissemination of best practices and support experimentation with locally adapted solutions. Collaboration among farmers, extension agents, researchers, and non-governmental organizations strengthens the capacity for innovation and scaling.

Enabling policies and institutional frameworks are crucial for creating an environment where sustainable intensification can thrive. Supportive policies may include research and development investments, incentives for EBS, risk-sharing mechanisms, and secure land tenure. Regulations that encourage the efficient use of resources, reduce barriers to innovation, and support market access further facilitate adoption.

Market incentives and value chains play a pivotal role in scaling. Certification schemes, payments for ecosystem services, and premium pricing for sustainably produced products provide financial rewards that encourage farmers to invest in sustainable practices. Access to input and output markets, financial services, and infrastructure is also necessary for scaling up.

Monitoring, evaluation, and adaptive management underpin the successful expansion of sustainable intensification. Collecting data on yields, resource use, ecosystem services, and social outcomes enables stakeholders to assess progress, identify barriers, and adjust strategies as needed.

Integrating sustainable intensification into national and regional agricultural strategies aligns public and private investments with long-term sustainability goals. Partnerships between governments, civil society, the private sector, and farmers' organizations can drive coordinated action at scale.

Achieving widespread adoption of sustainable intensification practices creates resilient, productive, and environmentally sound food systems capable of meeting present and future challenges. The scaling process builds a foundation for global food security and ecosystem health.

Chapter 8: Landscape Approaches and Connectivity

Chapter 8 highlights the significance of landscape approaches and ecological connectivity in shaping resilient and sustainable agricultural regions. Recognizing that ecological processes—such as species movement, water flow, and nutrient cycling—extend beyond individual farms, this chapter explores strategies for managing agriculture at the landscape scale. It examines the creation of landscape mosaics, the role of corridors for species movement and gene flow, and the value of watershed and catchment-based approaches. Emphasis is placed on coordinating efforts across farms and jurisdictions, fostering governance and stakeholder collaboration, and applying principles that balance production with conservation. By integrating EBS into broader landscape planning, Chapter 8 demonstrates how connectivity enhances biodiversity, supports ecosystem services, and strengthens the long-term productivity and health of agricultural systems.

Principles of Landscape-Scale Management

Landscape-scale management is an approach that considers agricultural fields, natural habitats, water resources, and human activities as interconnected components within a larger landscape. This perspective recognizes that many ecological processes—such as nutrient cycling, water movement, species migration, and pest regulation—operate across broader spatial scales than a single farm or field. Managing at the landscape level supports ecosystem function, agricultural productivity, and biodiversity conservation simultaneously.

One key principle is the integration of multiple land uses and objectives. Rather than maximizing one output, such as crop yield, landscape-scale management balances food production with the provision of ecosystem services, including water regulation, carbon storage, habitat conservation, and cultural values. This involves mapping landscape features, identifying priority areas for conservation, and designing multifunctional spaces that serve various needs.

Connectivity is another guiding principle. Maintaining or restoring corridors, hedgerows, riparian buffers, and patches of natural habitat ensures the movement of species and the flow of ecological processes across the landscape. Connectivity enhances pollination, natural pest control, and resilience to environmental disturbances.

Collaboration among stakeholders is essential at the landscape scale. Landowners, farmers, communities, conservation organizations, and policymakers must coordinate their actions to achieve shared goals. Participatory planning and inclusive decision-making foster ownership, reduce conflicts, and align efforts for greater impact.

Adaptive management underpins landscape-scale approaches. Because landscapes are dynamic and complex, management strategies must be flexible, responsive to monitoring data, and open to adjustment as conditions change or new information emerges.

Monitoring and evaluation at the landscape level provide feedback on the effectiveness of management actions and help identify opportunities for improvement. Data on land use, ecosystem services, biodiversity, and social outcomes support informed decision-making and accountability.

Enabling policies, incentives, and technical support are required to sustain landscape-scale management. These mechanisms encourage practices that benefit both agriculture and the environment, making it feasible and attractive for land managers to participate.

Applying the principles of landscape-scale management creates resilient agricultural systems embedded in healthy, functioning ecosystems, delivering benefits that extend beyond individual farms to entire regions and communities.

Landscape Mosaics and Ecological Networks

Landscape mosaics and ecological networks are foundational concepts in the management of agricultural landscapes for both productivity and biodiversity. A landscape mosaic refers to the patchwork of different land uses, habitats, and management practices that exist within a given area—such as crop fields, pastures, woodlands, wetlands, and built environments. Ecological networks connect these patches, enabling the movement of species, the flow of genetic material, and the functioning of ecosystem processes across the broader landscape.

The diversity and arrangement of patches in a landscape mosaic influence how organisms use the land, access resources, and interact with each other. Diverse mosaics with well-integrated natural habitats—such as hedgerows, buffer strips, forest patches, and ponds—provide shelter, food, and migration corridors for a wide array of species. This connectivity supports pollinators, pest predators, and other beneficial organisms, ultimately enhancing crop productivity and ecological stability.

Ecological networks, created by linking habitat patches through corridors and stepping stones, are essential for the survival of many species. These networks mitigate the effects of habitat fragmentation, allowing wildlife to move in response to seasonal changes, resource availability, or environmental stressors. Connectivity also facilitates gene flow, which is crucial for the adaptation and resilience of populations facing changing conditions.

In agricultural landscapes, designing and maintaining landscape mosaics and ecological networks requires strategic planning. Identifying and preserving key habitat patches, restoring degraded areas, and establishing corridors ensure that agricultural intensification does not come at the expense of biodiversity and ecosystem function. Functional networks also help buffer farms against pest outbreaks and climate extremes by supporting a diversity of natural enemies and resilient ecological processes.

The participation of multiple landowners and stakeholders is often necessary to create and maintain effective mosaics and networks. Collaborative approaches ensure that actions taken on individual farms contribute to broader landscape-level goals.

Promoting landscape mosaics and ecological networks strengthens the ecological infrastructure of farming regions, supporting sustainable production and long-term environmental health. These concepts provide a blueprint for integrating agriculture and conservation across spatial scales.

Corridors for Species Movement and Gene Flow

Corridors for species movement and gene flow are vital elements in agricultural landscapes designed to sustain biodiversity and ecosystem function. Corridors are strips or patches of natural or semi-natural habitat—such as hedgerows, riparian zones, grassy field margins, or connected woodlots—that link larger habitat areas and allow organisms to move freely across the landscape. Their primary role is to overcome the effects of habitat fragmentation caused by intensive agriculture, infrastructure development, or land conversion.

Species movement through corridors enables animals, insects, and even plants (via pollinators or seed dispersers) to access resources, find mates, migrate seasonally, and recolonize areas after disturbances. This connectivity is essential for maintaining healthy wildlife populations and supporting ecological processes such as pollination and pest regulation.

Gene flow, the exchange of genetic material between populations, is equally important for the resilience of species. Corridors facilitate the movement of individuals between otherwise isolated populations, increasing genetic diversity and adaptive capacity. Higher genetic diversity allows species to better withstand disease, climate variability, and environmental change, reducing the risk of local extinctions.

Designing effective corridors requires attention to width, length, habitat quality, and connectivity to existing natural areas. Wider corridors and those with diverse native vegetation offer more resources and greater protection for species moving through them. Corridors should be planned to connect core habitats, such as forests, wetlands, or grasslands, and avoid barriers like roads or intensively managed fields whenever possible.

Corridors also provide co-benefits for farms. They attract beneficial insects, birds, and bats that contribute to pest control and pollination, supporting agricultural productivity. Vegetated corridors stabilize soils, reduce runoff, and improve water quality by filtering sediments and nutrients before they reach waterways.

The establishment and maintenance of corridors often require collaboration among landowners, conservation groups, and policymakers to ensure that connectivity goals are met at a meaningful scale. Participatory planning and incentives can support corridor creation and long-term stewardship.

By incorporating corridors for species movement and gene flow, agricultural landscapes become more permeable, ecologically functional, and capable of supporting both productive farming and vibrant biodiversity.

Coordinating Across Farms and Jurisdictions

Coordinating across farms and jurisdictions is essential for effective landscape-scale management in agricultural regions, as ecological processes and challenges rarely conform to property or administrative boundaries. Issues such as water management, pest migration, habitat connectivity, and nutrient cycling often extend well beyond the limits of individual farms, requiring collaborative solutions among neighboring landowners, communities, and governmental entities.

Successful coordination begins with shared recognition of landscape-level objectives—such as maintaining ecosystem services, conserving biodiversity, reducing pollution, or mitigating climate risks. Stakeholders need mechanisms for regular communication, joint planning, and the development of common goals that reflect the interests and responsibilities of all parties involved.

Watershed management is a classic example of cross-boundary coordination. Farmers, local governments, and water users work together to manage water resources, control runoff, and protect water quality across the entire catchment area. Similarly, collaborative efforts in managing pest outbreaks or invasive species benefit from synchronized actions—such as the timing of crop planting, pest monitoring, or the establishment of habitat corridors—across multiple properties.

Jurisdictional coordination may involve aligning policies, regulations, and incentives at local, regional, or national levels. Land use planning, zoning, and conservation programs that support multifunctional landscapes and ecological connectivity are more effective when developed in consultation with a broad array of stakeholders. Funding and technical assistance can be directed to support collective action and innovation.

Participatory approaches, such as farmer groups, cooperatives, community associations, or public-private partnerships, strengthen social networks and resource sharing. These platforms facilitate knowledge exchange, mutual support, and adaptive management, allowing stakeholders to address emerging challenges together.

Transparency, trust, and equitable participation are key to long-term success. Ensuring that all voices are heard, benefits are fairly distributed, and conflicts are resolved constructively helps build a strong foundation for ongoing collaboration.

Coordinated action across farms and jurisdictions enhances the effectiveness of EBS, supporting landscape-scale resilience, agricultural productivity, and environmental health. This integrated approach helps regions respond to complex challenges, harness shared opportunities, and create multifunctional landscapes that serve both people and nature.

Watershed and Catchment-Based Approaches

Watershed and catchment-based approaches recognize that water flows and ecological processes operate across natural landscape boundaries rather than administrative or property lines. A watershed—or catchment—is an area of land where all precipitation collects and drains to a common outlet, such as a river, lake, or wetland. Managing agricultural systems within the context of entire watersheds provides a holistic framework for addressing water quality, quantity, and ecosystem health.

This approach starts with understanding the interconnectedness of upland, lowland, and aquatic environments. Land use practices, soil management, and vegetation cover in one part of the watershed can have downstream effects on water availability, sediment loads, and pollutant transport. Agricultural activities—such as tillage, irrigation, fertilization, and livestock management—are coordinated to minimize negative impacts and support the overall function of the watershed.

Implementing best management practices across the watershed includes maintaining vegetative buffers along waterways, restoring wetlands, and promoting soil conservation measures that reduce erosion and runoff. These interventions protect water quality by filtering sediments, nutrients, and chemicals before they reach streams and rivers. Integrated water management strategies, such as water harvesting, efficient irrigation, and groundwater recharge, help balance water supply and demand throughout the catchment.

Watershed and catchment-based approaches require collaboration among diverse stakeholders—farmers, communities, industry, local authorities, and environmental organizations. Participatory planning processes build consensus on shared goals, coordinate actions, and ensure that upstream and downstream interests are balanced. These efforts are supported by data collection, monitoring, and adaptive management to track progress and respond to new challenges.

Policy frameworks, financial incentives, and technical assistance facilitate the adoption of watershed-based management. Integrated planning aligns agricultural production with conservation and climate adaptation objectives, making the most efficient use of resources while sustaining ecosystem services.

Approaching agriculture through the lens of the watershed or catchment creates resilient landscapes that buffer against floods and droughts, support biodiversity, and ensure clean water for farming and communities alike. This systems perspective strengthens the sustainability and productivity of agricultural regions in the long term.

Monitoring and Evaluating Landscape Function

Monitoring and evaluating landscape function are vital for ensuring that ecosystem-based management delivers its intended outcomes in agricultural regions. Landscape function refers to the ability of the land to sustain ecosystem processes such as nutrient cycling, water regulation, habitat provision, and the maintenance of biodiversity— all of which support productive agriculture and environmental health.

A systematic approach to monitoring begins with identifying clear objectives, indicators, and baseline conditions. Common indicators include soil health (organic matter content, structure, erosion rates), water quality (nutrient loads, sediment, chemical contaminants), biodiversity (species richness and abundance), and land cover change. Socioeconomic indicators, such as farm income, employment, or community well-being, may also be tracked to assess broader impacts.

Remote sensing, satellite imagery, geographic information systems (GIS), and field-based surveys are valuable tools for collecting and analyzing data at multiple spatial and temporal scales. Regular assessments detect changes in land use, vegetation cover, and ecological connectivity, providing early warning of degradation or improvements.

Participatory monitoring involves farmers, landowners, and communities in data collection and interpretation, fostering local ownership and adaptive management. This collaborative approach helps tailor monitoring programs to local priorities and ensures that results are accessible and relevant to stakeholders.

Evaluation interprets the data collected through monitoring, comparing observed trends to management goals and benchmarks. Understanding what works, what doesn't, and why allows for the refinement of management practices and policies. Feedback loops—where results inform decisions and adjustments—are fundamental to adaptive landscape management.

Challenges in monitoring and evaluation include limited resources, technical capacity, and coordination among stakeholders. Addressing these barriers requires investment in training, technology, and partnerships, as well as supportive policies that encourage transparency and data sharing.

Effective monitoring and evaluation build accountability, guide investment, and support the scaling up of successful EBS. These processes are critical for achieving resilient, multifunctional landscapes that sustain both agricultural productivity and the natural resources on which farming depends.

Governance and Stakeholder Collaboration

Governance and stakeholder collaboration are central to effective landscape-scale management and the success of ecosystem-based agricultural solutions. Governance encompasses the policies, institutions, decision-making processes, and power dynamics that shape how resources are managed, benefits are distributed, and responsibilities are shared across the landscape. Strong, inclusive governance creates the enabling conditions for sustainable agriculture, environmental stewardship, and rural development.

Collaborative governance involves engaging a diverse range of stakeholders—farmers, landowners, local communities, government agencies, conservation organizations, private sector actors, and researchers—in decision-making and implementation. Each stakeholder brings unique perspectives, knowledge, and resources, contributing to holistic and context-appropriate solutions.

Transparent, participatory processes ensure that all voices are heard, fostering trust, legitimacy, and shared ownership of outcomes. Stakeholder mapping and analysis help identify interests, potential conflicts, and synergies, guiding the design of inclusive forums and negotiation platforms. Regular dialogue, joint planning, and collective problem-solving enable stakeholders to align goals, coordinate actions, and address complex challenges that cross boundaries and jurisdictions.

Institutional frameworks—such as watershed committees, farmer cooperatives, public-private partnerships, or community-based organizations—provide mechanisms for coordination, accountability, and adaptive management. Clear rules, incentives, and dispute resolution mechanisms support effective collaboration and long-term commitment.

Multi-level governance recognizes that decisions affecting the landscape often involve actors at different scales, from local to national or even international levels. Vertical and horizontal integration of policies, programs, and investments ensures coherence and maximizes impact.

Capacity building, technical assistance, and knowledge exchange are essential for empowering stakeholders to participate meaningfully.

Access to information, training, and financial resources strengthens the ability of all groups—especially marginalized or resource-poor actors—to engage in governance processes and benefit from EBS.

Monitoring, evaluation, and learning support adaptive governance by tracking progress, sharing lessons, and informing continuous improvement. Flexibility and willingness to adjust strategies as conditions change or new opportunities arise enhance the resilience of governance systems.

Effective governance and stakeholder collaboration deliver multifunctional landscapes that balance agricultural productivity, environmental conservation, and social well-being. This approach supports the long-term viability of rural communities and secures the ecosystem services on which they depend.

Chapter 9: Enabling Policies and Institutional Support

Chapter 9 examines the critical role of enabling policies and institutional support in advancing EBS within agriculture. The successful adoption and scaling of EBS depend not only on individual farm practices but also on the wider policy environment, effective governance, and strong institutions at multiple levels. This chapter explores policy frameworks, incentives, and regulatory mechanisms that promote sustainable agriculture, as well as the importance of secure land tenure, access to financing, and stakeholder collaboration. It highlights how multilateral, national, and local institutions contribute to the development, implementation, and mainstreaming of EBS. By analyzing the integration of Indigenous and local knowledge, research and development, and participatory governance, Chapter 9 provides practical insights into creating the supportive systems needed to embed EBS across diverse agricultural landscapes.

Policy Frameworks for Ecosystem-Based Agriculture

Policy frameworks for ecosystem-based agriculture are designed to create an enabling environment that supports the widespread adoption and scaling of ecological practices in farming. These frameworks set the direction for how governments, institutions, and stakeholders integrate biodiversity, ecosystem services, and sustainable resource management into agricultural policy and planning.

A robust policy framework begins with clear national or regional strategies that prioritize sustainable agriculture, climate resilience, and environmental protection alongside food security and rural development. Such strategies typically set out goals for conserving natural resources, restoring degraded lands, and supporting livelihoods, forming the basis for regulations, incentives, and investment.

Regulatory measures play an important role in protecting ecosystem services and guiding land use. Environmental impact assessments, land zoning, buffer requirements, and restrictions on the use of certain agrochemicals help ensure that farming activities do not compromise water quality, soil health, or biodiversity. Policies that support the establishment and protection of natural habitats, such as wetlands, forests, and riparian zones, reinforce the ecological foundation of agriculture.

Incentive mechanisms—including payments for ecosystem services, subsidies, tax benefits, and access to technical assistance— encourage farmers to adopt practices such as conservation tillage, agroforestry, and cover cropping. Certification schemes, eco-labels, and sustainable sourcing requirements from the private sector further promote ecosystem-based approaches and reward farmers for stewardship.

Research, extension, and education policies are central to building capacity and driving innovation. Investments in farmer training, participatory research, and advisory services ensure that knowledge about ecosystem-based practices reaches rural communities and is adapted to local contexts.

Effective policy frameworks also require coordination across sectors, such as agriculture, water, forestry, and environment, to ensure coherence and avoid conflicting mandates. Cross-sectoral collaboration, stakeholder engagement, and adaptive governance help align interests and resources.

Regular monitoring, evaluation, and feedback ensure that policy frameworks remain relevant, effective, and responsive to changing conditions and scientific knowledge. Transparent processes for stakeholder input and revision promote shared ownership and accountability.

Comprehensive policy frameworks empower farmers and rural communities to integrate EBS, contributing to resilient food systems, environmental health, and sustainable development.

Incentives and Support Mechanisms for EBS Adoption

Incentives and support mechanisms are vital for accelerating the adoption of EBS in agriculture, helping farmers overcome financial, technical, and informational barriers. By aligning economic rewards and institutional support with sustainable practices, these mechanisms encourage the transition from conventional approaches to farming systems that prioritize ecosystem health and resilience.

Financial incentives play a prominent role in promoting EBS. Payments for ecosystem services (PES) reward farmers for activities that deliver public benefits—such as improved water quality, enhanced biodiversity, carbon sequestration, or flood mitigation. Direct subsidies, grants, and cost-sharing programs help offset the initial expenses of adopting new technologies or practices, such as cover cropping, agroforestry, or the establishment of buffer strips. Tax credits and reductions in land or water use fees further reduce the financial burden of implementing EBS.

Market-based incentives, including certification schemes and eco-labels, allow producers to access premium markets and receive higher prices for sustainably produced goods. Contracts with buyers or processors that specify sustainability requirements can create stable demand for products grown using EBS.

Technical support is equally important. Extension services, advisory programs, and farmer field schools provide training, knowledge exchange, and hands-on guidance for planning, implementing, and managing EBS. Demonstration sites and farmer-to-farmer networks enable producers to learn from local experiences and adapt practices to their own contexts.

Access to credit, insurance, and risk-sharing instruments helps farmers manage uncertainty and invest in long-term sustainability. Innovative financing options—such as green bonds or revolving funds—can channel resources into landscape restoration or regenerative agriculture projects.

Policy support and regulatory frameworks create an enabling environment for EBS adoption. Streamlined permitting, flexible land use regulations, and recognition of EBS in subsidy or incentive programs encourage wider uptake.

Information dissemination, participatory research, and monitoring systems empower farmers to make informed decisions and track the benefits of EBS adoption. Inclusive stakeholder engagement ensures that support mechanisms address the needs of diverse producers, including smallholders and marginalized groups.

Effective incentives and support mechanisms catalyze the transformation of agriculture, making EBS accessible, attractive, and viable for producers at all scales.

Mainstreaming EBS in National and Regional Strategies

Mainstreaming EBS in national and regional strategies is essential for embedding ecological approaches into the core of agricultural policy, planning, and development. When EBS become an integral part of strategy documents and action plans, governments and institutions signal a commitment to sustainable, resilient, and climate-smart agriculture.

Incorporating EBS into overarching agricultural, environmental, and rural development strategies ensures coherence across sectors. Clear policy goals—such as conserving biodiversity, restoring degraded landscapes, enhancing water management, and supporting climate adaptation—set the foundation for prioritizing EBS at all levels of planning and investment.

Strategic frameworks should outline specific targets, timelines, and indicators for EBS implementation. This enables monitoring of progress, accountability, and transparent reporting. Aligning EBS with international commitments—such as the Sustainable Development Goals (SDGs), Paris Agreement, and biodiversity conventions—strengthens policy relevance and attracts global support and funding.

Cross-sectoral integration is critical. Coordination among agriculture, environment, water, forestry, and finance ministries avoids conflicting mandates and maximizes synergies. Joint task forces, inter-ministerial committees, and multi-stakeholder platforms facilitate dialogue and collaboration, ensuring that EBS objectives are mainstreamed across policy areas.

Resource allocation must reflect EBS priorities. Budget lines for ecosystem restoration, agroecology, and landscape management should be established within national and regional budgets. Investment in research, capacity building, and extension services accelerates the spread of EBS knowledge and practice.

Decentralization and local empowerment are important for effective mainstreaming. Regional and local authorities should be supported to tailor EBS strategies to specific contexts, ecosystems, and community needs. Participatory planning processes ensure that local stakeholders contribute to strategy development and implementation.

Public awareness campaigns and education programs reinforce the importance of EBS and build societal support. Demonstration projects, pilot programs, and knowledge-sharing networks showcase successful EBS models and provide templates for scaling up.

By mainstreaming EBS in national and regional strategies, countries lay the groundwork for transforming agricultural systems, protecting natural resources, and achieving resilient, productive landscapes that benefit both people and nature.

Integrating EBS into Agricultural Extension Services

Integrating EBS into agricultural extension services is a critical step toward widespread adoption of sustainable practices in farming communities. Extension services—through their direct engagement with farmers—play a key role in translating ecological concepts, scientific research, and policy into practical, actionable guidance on the ground.

To be effective, extension programs must equip advisors and field staff with up-to-date knowledge of EBS, including agroecology, soil health, water management, biodiversity conservation, and climate adaptation. Training and capacity building for extension personnel ensure that they can provide tailored, context-specific recommendations and demonstrate the practical benefits of ecosystem-based approaches.

Participatory extension methods are particularly valuable for promoting EBS. Engaging farmers in on-farm trials, demonstration plots, and farmer field schools fosters peer learning and experimentation. These interactive approaches allow producers to observe the results of EBS practices firsthand, adapt them to their own conditions, and share experiences with neighbors.

Integrating EBS into extension curricula and resource materials ensures that topics such as cover cropping, IPM, agroforestry, conservation tillage, and habitat creation become standard elements of advisory support. Digital tools, mobile applications, and online knowledge platforms expand the reach of extension services and facilitate the timely dissemination of information on EBS.

Extension services also act as a bridge between research institutions, policymakers, and farmers. By gathering feedback from the field, extension staff inform research agendas and policy development, ensuring that EBS innovations address real-world challenges and farmer priorities.

Special attention should be paid to reaching marginalized and smallholder farmers, who may face barriers to accessing extension services and adopting new practices. Inclusive approaches—such as gender-sensitive programming and targeted outreach—help ensure equitable participation and benefits from EBS adoption.

Institutional support, adequate funding, and continuous professional development for extension agencies are vital for sustaining the integration of EBS. Monitoring and evaluation systems help assess the effectiveness of extension activities and inform ongoing improvements.

Embedding EBS into agricultural extension services accelerates the transition toward regenerative and resilient agriculture, empowering farmers to steward their land for long-term productivity and environmental health.

Land Tenure, Rights, and Access

Land tenure, rights, and access are foundational issues for the successful implementation of EBS in agriculture. Secure and equitable land tenure determines who can use land, make decisions about its management, invest in long-term sustainability, and benefit from improvements. When farmers and communities have clear, legally recognized rights to their land and resources, they are more likely to adopt practices that support ecosystem health and resilience.

Uncertain or insecure land tenure often discourages investment in EBS, as farmers may fear losing their land or not being able to reap the long-term benefits of their stewardship. This insecurity can be especially pronounced among women, smallholders, Indigenous peoples, and marginalized groups, who may lack formal documentation or recognition of customary rights. Addressing these disparities is crucial for ensuring inclusive and effective EBS adoption.

Policies that formalize and protect land rights—through titling, registration, or recognition of customary and communal tenure— help create the stability needed for sustainable land management. Transparent, accessible processes for resolving disputes, mediating conflicts, and clarifying overlapping claims further support secure tenure.

Access to land is equally important. Barriers such as high land costs, restrictive inheritance laws, or discriminatory practices can prevent individuals and communities from participating in ecosystem-based agriculture. Land reform programs, redistribution schemes, and targeted support for disadvantaged groups can enhance access and foster more equitable participation.

Tenure security must also extend to water, forests, and other natural resources critical for EBS. Integrated resource rights, such as community-based management or joint tenure arrangements, can strengthen stewardship and facilitate coordinated landscape management.

Ensuring the rights and participation of women and underrepresented groups is vital for achieving inclusive and sustainable outcomes. Gender-sensitive policies, joint titling, and capacity building empower all land users to contribute to and benefit from EBS.

Institutions, laws, and programs that support secure tenure and equitable access underpin the social foundation of ecosystem-based agriculture. When land users feel confident in their rights, they are better positioned to invest in regenerative practices, conserve resources, and build resilient landscapes for future generations.

Financing and Investment in EBS

Financing and investment are critical to the successful adoption and scaling of EBS in agriculture. Implementing EBS often requires upfront capital, ongoing maintenance, and technical assistance—costs that can be a barrier for farmers, especially smallholders and marginalized communities. Effective financial mechanisms and investment strategies help bridge this gap, making EBS accessible and attractive to a wide range of producers.

Public funding remains an essential source of support for EBS. Government programs can provide grants, subsidies, or cost-sharing arrangements for activities such as habitat restoration, agroforestry, conservation tillage, and water harvesting. These funds lower the financial risks for farmers adopting new practices and signal a broader policy commitment to sustainable agriculture.

Private investment also plays an increasing role. Impact investors, agri-businesses, and financial institutions are recognizing the value of EBS in delivering long-term returns through improved soil health, climate resilience, and ecosystem services. Loans, equity investments, and blended finance models can channel private capital into projects that generate both financial and environmental benefits.

Innovative financial instruments—such as green bonds, sustainability-linked loans, and payments for ecosystem services (PES)—reward farmers and land managers for delivering positive environmental outcomes. PES schemes compensate producers for activities that improve water quality, sequester carbon, or conserve biodiversity, providing new revenue streams that encourage adoption of EBS.

Access to credit and insurance is also crucial. Affordable, flexible loans help cover the costs of transitioning to EBS, while weather-indexed insurance and risk-sharing products protect farmers from climate-related shocks. These tools build financial resilience and support long-term sustainability.

Partnerships among governments, financial institutions, NGOs, and producer organizations can create funding pools and technical assistance platforms tailored to local needs. Capacity building in financial literacy and business planning empowers farmers to access and manage investment effectively.

Transparent monitoring and reporting on the outcomes of EBS investments build confidence among funders, ensuring that resources are directed toward practices with proven benefits.

Strategic financing and investment enable the widespread implementation of EBS, transforming agricultural landscapes and supporting resilient, sustainable food systems for the future.

Role of Multilateral, National, and Local Institutions

Multilateral, national, and local institutions all play vital roles in enabling the adoption, scaling, and sustainability of EBS in agriculture. These institutions shape the policy, financial, technical, and social environments in which EBS are developed and implemented, ensuring that diverse needs and contexts are addressed at every level.

Multilateral organizations—such as the United Nations, World Bank, Global Environment Facility, and regional development banks—set global agendas, provide funding, and foster cross-country knowledge exchange. Their support brings international visibility to ecosystem-based approaches, mobilizes resources for pilot projects and capacity building, and establishes standards and best practices that can be adapted locally. Multilateral agencies often help coordinate large-scale initiatives, promote science-based policy, and align EBS strategies with international agreements such as the Sustainable Development Goals (SDGs) and the Paris Agreement.

National governments translate international commitments into actionable policies, regulatory frameworks, and investment plans. Ministries of agriculture, environment, finance, and rural development are responsible for integrating EBS into national strategies, providing incentives, and facilitating research and extension services. National institutions also coordinate funding, establish monitoring systems, and ensure policy coherence across sectors.

Local institutions—such as municipal governments, farmer organizations, cooperatives, and community-based groups—are crucial for on-the-ground implementation and adaptation. These entities understand local contexts, manage natural resources, and engage directly with land users. Local governments support land use planning, zoning, and the delivery of extension and advisory services. Producer groups foster knowledge sharing, represent farmer interests, and support peer-to-peer learning and collective action.

Collaboration among these institutional levels is essential for success. Multilevel governance, joint planning, and regular dialogue ensure that policies and programs are responsive, context-appropriate, and equitable. Technical assistance, capacity building, and transparent monitoring facilitate the effective flow of information and resources.

Partnerships across institutions amplify impact and bridge the gap between policy and practice. They help ensure that EBS are mainstreamed into agricultural development, environmental conservation, and climate adaptation agendas.

Institutional support at all levels strengthens the enabling environment for EBS, empowering producers and communities to achieve resilient, sustainable, and productive agricultural systems.

Chapter 10: Knowledge Systems, Innovation, And Monitoring

Chapter 10 explores the role of knowledge systems, innovation, and monitoring in the successful implementation and scaling of EBS in agriculture. Effective transformation requires more than new practices—it depends on continuous learning, adaptive management, and inclusive sharing of information across communities, institutions, and sectors. This chapter examines how research and development, capacity building, farmer-led innovation, and digital tools contribute to advancing EBS. It also highlights the importance of participatory monitoring and evaluation, transparent communication of outcomes, and feedback mechanisms that drive improvement. By focusing on knowledge exchange, collaboration, and the application of data-driven approaches, Chapter 10 provides a roadmap for building resilient agricultural systems that can adapt and thrive in a rapidly changing world.

The Role of Indigenous and Local Knowledge

Indigenous and local knowledge plays a crucial role in the design and implementation of EBS in agriculture. Rooted in generations of direct experience and observation, this knowledge embodies a deep understanding of local ecosystems, climate patterns, soils, water cycles, plants, animals, and farming practices. Incorporating Indigenous and local perspectives enriches EBS approaches, ensuring they are context-specific, culturally relevant, and grounded in the realities of the landscapes where they are applied.

Traditional agricultural practices—such as shifting cultivation, agroforestry, water harvesting, and rotational grazing—demonstrate principles of resource stewardship, risk management, and ecosystem resilience. Many of these practices reflect sophisticated systems for maintaining soil fertility, conserving water, supporting biodiversity, and coping with variable weather, often relying on diversity, polyculture, and seasonal cycles.

Engaging Indigenous peoples and local communities as partners in EBS planning and implementation builds on this wealth of experience. Participatory approaches that respect, document, and integrate traditional knowledge strengthen the legitimacy and effectiveness of solutions. Co-creation processes facilitate the blending of scientific research and local insight, leading to innovative practices and adaptive management strategies that respond to changing conditions.

Recognition of Indigenous and customary rights over land, water, and resources is essential for enabling the full participation of local communities in EBS. Legal protections, support for community-based management, and the inclusion of traditional governance systems foster stewardship and investment in long-term sustainability.

Knowledge-sharing platforms, farmer-to-farmer networks, and community training further disseminate best practices and encourage innovation. Equitable partnerships ensure that the benefits of EBS are shared and that cultural values and identities are respected.

Challenges may arise from power imbalances, loss of traditional knowledge, or limited access to resources and decision-making. Addressing these barriers requires institutional support, inclusive policies, and ongoing dialogue.

Valuing and integrating Indigenous and local knowledge leads to more robust, resilient, and adaptive EBS in agriculture, benefiting both people and the environments they manage.

Research and Development in Agricultural EBS

Research and development (R&D) in agricultural EBS drive innovation, adaptation, and the evidence base needed for the widespread adoption of sustainable practices. Robust R&D programs generate knowledge, technologies, and management strategies that enhance productivity, resource efficiency, and ecological resilience in farming systems.

A key focus of EBS research is understanding the complex interactions among crops, soils, water, biodiversity, and climate within agricultural landscapes. Interdisciplinary studies integrate ecological, agronomic, economic, and social dimensions to identify best practices for building soil health, conserving water, supporting beneficial organisms, and reducing chemical inputs. Long-term field trials and landscape experiments help assess the performance and adaptability of EBS under diverse conditions.

Development of new tools and technologies—such as decision-support systems, remote sensing, soil health indicators, and improved crop varieties—facilitates the monitoring, planning, and management of ecosystem-based practices. Participatory research approaches that involve farmers, extension agents, and local communities ensure that innovations are practical, context-specific, and responsive to user needs.

EBS research also explores policy, institutional, and market barriers to adoption, identifying pathways to scale up solutions. Social science research contributes insights into farmer decision-making, knowledge exchange, and the social impacts of adopting EBS. Economic analyses assess the costs, benefits, and risk profiles associated with ecosystem-based practices, providing guidance for policymakers and investors.

Partnerships between universities, research institutes, the private sector, government agencies, and farmer organizations accelerate the pace of R&D. Collaborative networks and knowledge-sharing platforms foster the exchange of data, experiences, and successful models across regions.

Funding for EBS research is crucial, enabling sustained experimentation, capacity building, and technology transfer. Targeted investment in R&D programs supports the development and refinement of EBS tailored to different crops, environments, and farming systems.

Monitoring and evaluation of R&D outcomes help track progress, share lessons, and guide future research agendas. Continuous innovation and learning ensure that agricultural EBS remain effective and relevant as conditions change.

Advances in research and development underpin the transition to resilient, productive, and environmentally sound agricultural systems based on EBS.

Capacity Building and Farmer-Led Innovation

Capacity building and farmer-led innovation are essential drivers for the successful adoption and scaling of EBS in agriculture. When farmers have access to knowledge, skills, resources, and networks, they are empowered to experiment, adapt, and refine practices that fit their specific contexts, leading to more sustainable and resilient agricultural systems.

Capacity building encompasses a broad range of activities, including training programs, workshops, field demonstrations, extension services, and access to information resources. These initiatives equip farmers with the technical know-how needed to implement EBS, such as IPM, soil health improvement, water conservation, and habitat restoration. Continuous education ensures that farmers remain informed about new developments, tools, and best practices in ecosystem-based agriculture.

Farmer-led innovation places producers at the center of the adaptation and development process. Recognizing that farmers are experts in their own landscapes, this approach values their experience, observations, and creativity. On-farm experimentation, participatory research, and peer-to-peer learning foster the co-creation and dissemination of solutions that are practical, scalable, and grounded in real-world challenges.

Networks and farmer organizations play a key role in facilitating knowledge exchange, supporting collective action, and advocating for supportive policies. These platforms enable farmers to share success stories, troubleshoot problems, and build community resilience. Women, youth, and marginalized groups should be actively included in capacity building and innovation initiatives to ensure diverse perspectives and equitable access to benefits.

Access to resources—such as seeds, tools, credit, and information technologies—removes barriers to experimentation and adoption. Digital platforms and mobile applications can further expand the reach of capacity building, delivering timely advice and connecting farmers to experts and markets.

Extension services and advisory programs that are participatory, responsive, and tailored to local needs are vital for sustaining farmer-led innovation. Continuous feedback and adaptive management ensure that learning is ongoing and that EBS evolve with changing conditions.

Strengthening capacity and fostering farmer-led innovation create the foundation for widespread, effective, and enduring adoption of EBS, transforming agriculture into a force for resilience, sustainability, and environmental stewardship.

Digital Tools and Data-Driven Approaches

Digital tools and data-driven approaches are transforming the landscape of EBS in agriculture. Advances in information and communication technology enable farmers, advisors, and policymakers to access real-time data, make informed decisions, and manage land more efficiently and sustainably. By harnessing digital innovations, agricultural systems become more adaptive, precise, and capable of delivering both productivity and environmental outcomes.

Remote sensing technologies—such as satellites, drones, and sensors—provide detailed information on crop growth, soil moisture, nutrient status, pest outbreaks, and weather conditions. This data helps farmers monitor fields at fine scales, detect problems early, and target interventions more effectively. Digital mapping and geographic information systems (GIS) facilitate landscape-level planning, helping optimize the placement of buffer strips, wetlands, or habitat corridors to support ecosystem services.

Decision-support tools and farm management software integrate diverse data sources to guide day-to-day operations. These platforms can generate recommendations for irrigation scheduling, nutrient management, pest control, and crop selection, tailored to local conditions and climate forecasts. Artificial intelligence (AI) and machine learning further enhance the predictive capacity of these tools, identifying patterns and suggesting adaptive strategies.

Mobile applications and digital advisory services expand the reach of extension support, connecting farmers with expert advice, weather alerts, market information, and peer networks. These tools empower even smallholder farmers in remote regions to access timely, actionable knowledge on EBS.

Data-driven approaches also support monitoring, evaluation, and reporting. Automated data collection and analysis streamline the assessment of ecosystem health, resource use, and the impacts of EBS, enabling adaptive management and transparent communication with stakeholders, funders, and regulators.

Collaboration among technology developers, researchers, extension agencies, and farmer organizations ensures that digital innovations are user-friendly, relevant, and accessible to diverse users. Addressing challenges such as digital literacy, data privacy, and infrastructure gaps is essential for equitable access and impact.

Embracing digital tools and data-driven approaches accelerates the transition to sustainable, resilient agriculture, enabling precise implementation and continuous improvement of EBS across farms and landscapes.

Participatory Monitoring and Evaluation

Participatory monitoring and evaluation (PM&E) is an inclusive approach that involves farmers, local communities, extension agents, and other stakeholders directly in assessing the progress and effectiveness of EBS in agriculture. Unlike top-down assessment methods, PM&E recognizes the value of local knowledge, empowers participants, and ensures that monitoring and evaluation processes are relevant, transparent, and adaptable to real-world conditions.

At the heart of PM&E is the collaborative identification of objectives, indicators, and data collection methods. Stakeholders work together to define what success looks like—such as improved soil health, increased biodiversity, better water quality, or higher yields—and select indicators that reflect their priorities and values. This process builds consensus, fosters ownership, and enhances the legitimacy of findings.

Data collection is shared among participants. Farmers and community members contribute observations, maintain records, and participate in surveys or field assessments. Training in data gathering and analysis increases local capacity, builds technical skills, and ensures that monitoring activities are meaningful and sustained over time.

Regular reflection and joint analysis sessions provide opportunities to review results, discuss challenges, and adapt management practices based on evidence. These feedback loops facilitate continuous improvement, allowing strategies to be fine-tuned and innovations to be adopted or scaled up.

PM&E also supports social learning and collective action. By sharing insights and experiences, participants learn from one another, strengthen networks, and build resilience at the community and landscape levels. Inclusive participation—actively engaging women, youth, and marginalized groups—ensures that diverse perspectives shape decision-making and that benefits are equitably distributed.

Transparent reporting of findings builds trust among stakeholders, funders, and policymakers. Documenting lessons learned and sharing results widely encourages the spread of successful EBS approaches and helps inform policy and program development.

Institutional support, technical assistance, and ongoing facilitation are important for sustaining PM&E efforts. Investment in participatory approaches pays off through more relevant, effective, and enduring EBS.

Participatory monitoring and evaluation enable adaptive management, community empowerment, and the long-term success of EBS in agriculture, building pathways for resilient and sustainable food systems.

Communicating Outcomes and Lessons Learned

Communicating outcomes and lessons learned is a crucial component of successful EBS in agriculture. Transparent, effective communication ensures that knowledge gained from implementing and evaluating EBS is shared widely, supporting adaptive management, scaling up of best practices, and continuous improvement across the sector.

Clear communication begins with documenting both quantitative outcomes—such as yield changes, water savings, or biodiversity increases—and qualitative insights, including challenges encountered, adaptations made, and factors behind successes or setbacks. Case studies, field reports, and monitoring data should be presented in accessible formats, tailored to the needs of different audiences, such as farmers, policymakers, researchers, and funding organizations.

Engaging storytelling, visual tools, and participatory workshops help convey the practical realities of EBS, making technical information relatable and actionable. Visual documentation—through photos, videos, and infographics—brings field experiences to life and showcases tangible results. Farmer voices, testimonials, and community narratives lend authenticity and foster trust, encouraging peer-to-peer learning.

Knowledge-sharing platforms and networks amplify the reach of lessons learned. Online databases, webinars, newsletters, and field days enable the rapid exchange of information across regions and stakeholder groups. Interactive events, such as farmer-to-farmer exchanges and learning journeys, promote social learning and inspire wider adoption of EBS.

Communicating setbacks and challenges is equally important. Honest reflection on what did not work and why helps prevent repeated mistakes and supports adaptive management. Transparent discussion of trade-offs, resource needs, and context-specific factors informs more realistic expectations and better decision-making.

Feedback mechanisms—such as surveys, focus groups, and community meetings—enable stakeholders to contribute insights, ask questions, and shape ongoing communication efforts. Two-way communication builds relationships and strengthens networks for collective action.

Policy briefs, summary reports, and targeted recommendations help translate lessons learned into actionable guidance for decision-makers, driving supportive policies and investment in EBS.

Effective communication of outcomes and lessons learned not only supports project success but also accelerates the broader transition toward resilient, sustainable agricultural systems that deliver lasting benefits for people and the environment.

Scaling and Mainstreaming Agricultural EBS

Scaling and mainstreaming agricultural EBS is essential for transforming farming systems at local, national, and global levels. Moving beyond isolated demonstration projects to widespread adoption ensures that the benefits of EBS—such as improved resilience, resource efficiency, and biodiversity conservation—become the norm across agricultural landscapes.

A coordinated strategy for scaling EBS starts with supportive policy frameworks that embed ecosystem-based principles into agricultural development plans, land use policies, and climate adaptation strategies. Clear targets, incentives, and regulatory measures guide public and private investment toward sustainable practices. Integration of EBS into national curricula, research agendas, and extension services builds institutional capacity for long-term change.

Building multi-stakeholder partnerships amplifies impact. Collaboration among farmers, governments, research institutions, private sector actors, NGOs, and community organizations enables sharing of knowledge, resources, and responsibilities. Platforms for joint planning, innovation, and monitoring accelerate the spread of EBS and ensure practices are adapted to diverse contexts.

Investment in capacity building, farmer-led innovation, and knowledge exchange fuels scaling. Farmer field schools, participatory research, and demonstration sites create opportunities for hands-on learning and adaptation. Digital tools, mobile apps, and information platforms broaden access to technical guidance and connect producers with peer networks and markets.

Securing financial resources is vital. Blended finance, green bonds, payments for ecosystem services, and dedicated funding streams lower barriers to adoption, making EBS feasible for producers of all sizes. Transparent monitoring and reporting systems demonstrate impact, attract additional investment, and maintain accountability.

Scaling EBS requires attention to equity and inclusion. Efforts should ensure that smallholders, women, Indigenous peoples, and marginalized groups are engaged and benefit from the transition. Participatory processes and targeted support foster social acceptance and widespread uptake.

Mainstreaming EBS in agricultural policy, education, markets, and supply chains shifts incentives and norms at scale. Certification schemes, sustainable sourcing requirements, and public procurement policies create demand for products grown using ecosystem-based approaches.

Scaling and mainstreaming agricultural EBS generates resilient food systems, restores landscapes, and delivers environmental, economic, and social benefits. This transformation supports global efforts to address climate change, food security, and sustainable development.

Conclusion

Agricultural EBS represent a transformative paradigm shift for the world's food systems—one that balances productivity with stewardship, resilience, and long-term sustainability. As global agriculture faces intensifying pressures from climate change, resource depletion, biodiversity loss, and shifting socioeconomic demands, the adoption of EBS offers a path to secure food production while regenerating the natural resources on which all farming depends.

Throughout this book, the centrality of ecological principles has been explored across every aspect of agricultural management, from soil health and water use to biodiversity conservation and landscape-scale planning. EBS practices—such as cover cropping, conservation tillage, crop and landscape diversification, agroforestry, and IPM—demonstrate that ecological integrity and high yields are not mutually exclusive. By fostering diversity, building organic matter, protecting water, and supporting natural regulatory processes, EBS approaches help farms maintain productivity, adapt to changing conditions, and provide vital ecosystem services for society.

The successful implementation and scaling of EBS require enabling policy frameworks, supportive institutions, inclusive governance, and access to tailored financial and technical resources. Incentives, education, research, and extension services all play roles in accelerating adoption and fostering innovation. Participatory approaches—grounded in local and Indigenous knowledge—are essential for ensuring that solutions are context-specific, equitable, and effective. When farmers and communities are empowered to co-create and adapt practices, EBS become rooted in everyday management and sustained across generations.

Integration of EBS at landscape and watershed scales further amplifies impact. Coordinated action across farms, sectors, and jurisdictions supports ecological connectivity, water management, and biodiversity conservation. Monitoring, evaluation, and adaptive management ensure that successes and lessons learned are captured, driving continuous improvement and responsive innovation as conditions change.

Scaling and mainstreaming EBS demand cross-sectoral collaboration and leadership at all levels—from multilateral agencies and national governments to local institutions and farmer networks. Clear policy signals, supportive markets, equitable access to resources, and a culture of knowledge exchange underpin the transformation toward resilient, regenerative agricultural landscapes.

Looking ahead, the case for EBS in agriculture is stronger than ever. These approaches align food production with planetary boundaries and societal needs, contributing to climate mitigation, adaptation, and sustainable development. As more farmers, communities, and countries adopt and champion ecosystem-based practices, the potential exists to reverse degradation, restore landscapes, and ensure food security for future generations.

The transition to ecosystem-based agriculture is not without challenges. It requires investment, patience, innovation, and commitment. However, the rewards—productive farms, thriving ecosystems, resilient rural communities, and a healthier planet—are profound and enduring. Embracing EBS is not just a technical or policy decision, but a fundamental step toward building agricultural systems that nourish both people and the Earth.